Private Investigations

Private Investigations

A Guide for the Beginner

Edward J. Herdrich

Copyright © 2009 by Edward J. Herdrich.

ISBN: Hardcover   978-1-4415-8450-2
           Softcover   978-1-4415-8449-6

All rights reserved. No part of this book may be reproduced or transmitted in any form or by any means, electronic or mechanical, including photocopying, recording, or by any information storage and retrieval system, without permission in writing from the copyright owner.

This book was printed in the United States of America.

To order additional copies of this book, contact:
Xlibris Corporation
1-888-795-4274
www.Xlibris.com
Orders@Xlibris.com
68654

CONTENTS

An Introduction 7

Chapter One: De-Mystification, or The Reality Check..........................13

Chapter Two: The Private Detective Defined, or
How Do I Know If I'll Be a Good Investigator?................................20

Chapter Three: Service (of Process) with a Smile 40

    CASE FILES: A Simple Serve...50

Chapter Four: Locate Investigations 57

    CASE FILES: When Looking for Lost Loved Ones,
    Sometimes It Pays to Advertise 75

Chapter Five: Surveillance, A True Test of Patience and Persistence 78

Chapter Six: Undercover Operations 93

    CASE FILES: Blue Collar Detective:
    The Real World of Undercover Investigations 111

Chapter Seven: Ethics and Professionalism 118

Chapter Eight: A Word, or Two, on Report-Writing 121

Chapter Nine: Recommended Reading 128

    CASE FILES: Bringing a Family Back Together 132

    CASE FILES: A Pretext is Worth a Thousand Databases...............139

Index of Questions 147

Index of State Regulatory Authorities 153

Index 161

AN INTRODUCTION

The first matter to address in this introduction has to be with respect to honesty. Although I am the author of this particular text, I am by no means intending to say, imply, or pretend that I am the originator of all the information contained herein. In point of fact, much of this has been taught to me over years and from a variety of sources. Much as I might not like to admit it, I went about it the hard way. Certain things, such as surveillance techniques, were taught to me more than once as I went from private to public and back to private. And, while there were some slight variations in terminology and methods of training, for the most part, the lessons were the same. It is, therefore, important for me to express my gratitude to the numerous people in my past who equally deserve credit for some of the information in this work. I cannot say that I remember all those people, or where it is that they necessarily obtained their information from (there were numerous, now misplaced or disposed of, hand-outs), but I am truly grateful to the various instructors that I had who are substantially responsible for my success and much of the information in this text.

The second matter to address should be a brief bio so that you are comfortable that I know of what I speak. I received a Bachelor of Arts with a Double Major in Criminal Justice and English from the University of Illinois at Chicago and took some classes toward my Master's degree from Western Illinois University. I graduated from the Police Training Institute, Champaign-Urbana, Illinois. I was in the US Army Military Police Corps (Honorably Discharged), and worked AWOL Apprehension (locating AWOL and Deserter status personnel and returning them to military control), the Drug Suppression Team (similar in nature to a civilian narcotics unit), and the Special Reactions Team (similar in nature to a civilian S.W.A.T.). I first worked in this industry in 1984, and obtained my own license in 1994.

The words *private detective* or *private investigator* do not necessarily conjure the image of a professional in the minds of many. More often, images are generated from common references: *The Maltese Falcon, The Rockford Files, Simon and Simon, Murder She Wrote,* or *Magnum P.I.* And, while some people find there to be certain advantages in the misconceptions about the profession (people will believe almost anything if you're a private detective), one of the primary reasons for my approach to this text is to de-mystify my current profession for the sake of those desiring to pursue it.

This text does not, nor does it purport to, address every issue, circumstance, possibility, aspect or nuance of private investigations—that would take several volumes. The purpose of this book is to provide an introduction to private investigations for those seriously considering the possibility of entering the field. It is intended to be used in conjunction with classroom instruction from an experienced professional, and should not **ever** be considered an "everything you need to know" text that can make you ready to hit the streets. Despite what some other books might claim, there is no such text in existence.

This text is oriented to persons intending to enter the field in the State of Illinois. Many of the techniques discussed will be the same nationwide, but **you must research the laws, regulations, licensing requirements and related legal, procedural or regulatory bodies in your own state.** In the index, there is a list of the agencies to contact in each state or a notation that the profession is not regulated in a given state. Some states, such as Missouri (as of the date of this writing) do not regulate the profession. Others, such as California, Texas, Florida and New York, are similar to Illinois—if you don't get familiar with all the regulations, they'll be explained to you very clearly at a disciplinary hearing. In Illinois, you can learn all you need to know about our current regulations and our governing body (the Department of Financial and Professional Regulation, Division of Professional Regulation) at www.idfpr.com.

Certain subjects to be discussed, such as carrying a firearm or whether using pretexts is an acceptable practice, are a matter of personal choice. There are obviously laws and regulations within each investigator's area that would need to be followed, but beyond that there is the choice as to whether or not the investigator desires to avail himself of herself of a certain option. In these instances, the author does not intend to dictate right or wrong or disparage anyone who holds a different view. But, as I have learned from being in this industry since 1984 and have been known to say in my classes (and usually more than once), one of the inescapable truths about the mindset of every private detective is that *he or she is the only private detective who knows how to do it the right way.* And, yes, I can be just as guilty of slipping into that mindset at times. While many private detectives would not like to admit it, there's a cowboy mentality that permeates the industry. Currently, I'm holding to the idea that genome research will prove a genetic disposition.

It needs to be said that the business of private investigations is a business. A detective agency or an individual license holder needs to be versed in business as well as investigative matters. For those of you who are contemplating the option of getting your license and working for yourself, whether or not you intend to start an agency and hire other people, **learn about running a business.** Whether that education is formal or otherwise is not important; that you understand it is necessary to be a successful professional is vital. Certain states will require you to work under someone else prior to being able to get your own license, but whether or not this is a requirement, working at an agency for a year or so before you go out on your own is a good idea to learn both investigative techniques and something about what is involved with running this kind of business. Learning from someone else's success or mistakes is not as important as long as you are learning.

A private detective (in Illinois, the classification is Private Detective, other states will have another and perhaps more than one professional classification) is a professional. The amount of knowledge and skills required, and the kind of oversight by government bodies, unquestionably qualifies this as not simply another job. For the good and the bad of it, this is not the kind of employment that generally lends itself to casual, part-time work. There is some of that work in the industry (shopper-testing being probably the best example), but the majority of work a private detective performs requires full-time attention to detail, knowledge of the skills, and knowledge of the related areas of laws and regulations. There are those in academia and in more traditional criminal justice/law enforcement professions who believe the private detective should be relegated to the shadow of a darkened corner. My own experience is that the level of professionalism in this profession is no less, or greater, than in any other area of criminal justice. To those who define professionalism by a degree obtained, I would ask, why is it that there is an expectation of more thoroughly educated professionals in the field when almost no institutions of higher learning would consider adding a curriculum that addresses the profession? I can say with confidence that developing a curriculum would not be too difficult. Courses could be, for instance, *Privatization and the Criminal Justice Professional, Criminal Law and Procedure; Civil Code and Procedure; Private Investigations, a History of the Profession; Case Management; Private Investigations—Laws and Regulations;* and *Private and Public Sector Cooperation and Coordination.* Coupled with some business classes, developing a program that addressed the profession appropriately would only leave out that that can't be taught in the classroom, and that is true of most professions that are associated with higher education.

An important point to make is that this text is concerned with *private investigations,* **not** *private security.* Providing security officers, equipment or services is also a respectable profession, but it is one that is distinctly different. In Illinois, there is in fact a separate license classification, separate training requirements, and different authorized operations. Those persons who are intending to enter the profession in the State of Illinois should also know that there is no legal classification of investigator. What you will find, though, is that most agencies and people within the industry in general tend to use the term investigator as designating someone who is working for an agency and who does not yet have his or her private detective license.

I have included within the text some short stories. These are non-fiction, and some of these have been previously published in *PI Magazine.* I include them because they will hopefully allow you to get a better sense of how the business can be in the reality, as opposed to the classroom. Of course, I do hope you'll find them entertaining as well as informative. Please know names and locations have been changed in these stories to protect the confidentiality of clients.

A last author's note. This text is intended for persons contemplating entering the field, but you may find that there are instances in that I will refer to you consulting with a client. If you are reading this text as that entry level person, you will most often not be having direct contact with the clients initially, except in the case of undercover operations. Where I make these references, know that the entry level investigator will be bringing these questions to a boss/supervisor, who will then consult with the client.

Although you may not be directly contacting the client, it is still important for you to understand the necessity of doing so.

Now, if you're ready for a straight-forward, practical look at getting into this line of work, please read on. I should quickly mention that, just as I do in my classes, you may see certain points repeated—this is intentional. You'll be happy to learn that one of the best things about this industry is that there is enough variety of work to satisfy just about anyone's disposition. This book cannot make you an effective investigator, nor can any course promise you success. But, by the time you have completed reading this text, you'll know whether the idea is still appealing, or if you need to return your Fedora and trench coat.

Author's Note: The pictures on the cover of this text are of the same person. They were taken approximately five minutes apart. The idea of disguise, while it is necessary at times, is no more complex than what is shown here. For the good, or bad of it depending upon your perspective, you may be appearing in various ways for work. But, as the back cover illustrates, there is a time and place for a more conventional look also.

CHAPTER ONE

De-Mystification, or The Reality Check

A shot rang out. I slammed the stick into fourth, cutting the wheel sharply, tires squealing from a turn taken too sharply. Around the corner, I stomped on the brakes. As the car slid to a stop, my left hand moved to open the door, while my right drifted up to the familiar weight of my forty-five. I slipped out of the car, liquid movement taking cold steel to its target.

This is a much more exciting scene than most anyone I know in the industry is likely to face, unless of course they welcome the possibility of being shot, and/or arrested, and/or civilly sued. As a matter of introducing you to this profession, I feel one of my first responsibilities is to eliminate some of the myths, even if some of them are generated from within the industry. In doing so, I do not intend to create an image of a boring profession but rather to put the emphasis where it belongs. The best private detectives are people who solve puzzles, who find unconventional solutions to problems that appear to have no solution, who know that one of the advantages we have over traditional law enforcement-oriented criminal justice practitioners is that we are not responding to emergencies where *cuffing and stuffing* is going to be a concern. If you are someone who is motivated by the possibility of detaining people, of hand-cuffing people, or similar *excitement*, you would be better served to look into private security. There are certain areas in the private detective profession that might involve these things, but they are by far in the minority.

Ex-cops, ninjas and soldiers of fortune. One of the questions I am frequently asked is, *don't you have to be an ex-cop or have military experience to get in the field?* While it is true that those experiences can be helpful in certain types of investigations, and for some people the military does attempt to instill certain qualities that are desirable, the truth is that a background of that nature is no more or less likely to ensure your success than one in accounting, insurance or even sales. Certainly, if you desire to specialize in Criminal Defense investigations, having law enforcement experience and/or a Criminal Justice degree would give you an edge over people who don't. Being out on the street working is at least as valuable as most classroom education when you actually have to conduct the investigation. Alternately, the person with formal education on the same subject may know better how to complete the investigation without crossing any lines that could put him, the attorney or the defendant in a position of having to be nervous about what gets presented in the courtroom. The reality, though, is that either one of those backgrounds and even having both might not be very useful unless you're performing certain types of investigations.

At an entry level, however, it is unlikely that most investigators would be put in charge of completing a criminal defense investigation. Working on certain aspects of the investigation might happen, but within dictated limitations. Whether in reference to criminal defense investigations, or simply examining the majority of work done in the field, there is no absolute better experience that can prepare you. Given that you might be working surveillance (sitting in a van for eight to twelve hours a day to determine if someone filed a false workers' compensation claim, or is cheating on his or her spouse), serving court papers, doing research at a courthouse, or working undercover at a worksite, it would be impossible for anyone to tell you exactly what type of background you need. This is a good thing because, simply put, it means that the diversity of work may require certain skills or qualities of a person but rarely a specific background.

A last word (almost) on the subject. In reference to self defense, it is conceivable that you may need to know some self-defense. Certain types of work—Executive Protection, Bail Enforcement, and similar assignments—require it unquestionably. However, even though I have a military police background, advanced firearms training, as well as related other training, I would be the first one to tell you that the best investigators are the ones who are capable of talking themselves out of almost any situation, or smart enough to plan ahead to avoid them.

What about the unexpected? The unexpected here is no more frequent or more dangerous than anywhere else—unless you lack that important quality, common sense. It has been my experience that most of the people who frequently face trouble of the type that requires self-defense, firearms, or similar training, are not facing the unexpected, but rather are facing the results of their own confrontational nature that escalates circumstances as opposed to diffusing hostilities.

Rockford, Magnum, et al. While I must confess that there is more than one television private detective I have liked over the years, and Dashiel Hammett's characters will remain a part of my movie and book libraries for the foreseeable future, in addressing the subject here we must speak to the fact that they are many steps removed from reality. Even Dashiel Hammett, who was a Pinkerton's man for twenty-some years, recognized that the exaggerations were necessary because the reality was not as likely to fascinate as the fiction would. Would you really want to watch a movie about a private detective sitting in the back of a van, waiting for a subject to bend over in a way that he allegedly can't due to an injury, or to read a book about a criminal defense investigation where the private detective didn't find a startling discovery but rather through persistence obtained statements that contradicted evidence, or even worse, watch a weekly series where the private detective went regularly to the Clerk of the Circuit Court's Office to check the criminal and civil background of employment or rental applicants?

Fiction is certainly fun, but it is at times nothing short of ridiculous. Someone, for instance, shooting a forty-five one handed while driving erratically in a Ferrari is ridiculous. Actually hitting the target instead of his or her own or another, uninvolved vehicle is just stupid. The lone operator who takes on the mob single-handedly and wins is ridiculous. The little old lady who just happens to know as much about poisons as she does about legal documents or interview techniques or whatever is important to that week's installment is ridiculous. These and the many other characterizations of movies, novels and television should all be approached from the same perspective. A brief side note for those who don't know it: the Sherlock Holmes created by Sir Arthur Conan Doyle had a drug addiction that sustained his ability to learn as much as he did, and it was Doctor Watson who, rather than being the bumbling oaf presented in movies, was responsible for handling the practical matters.

Luck and the scientific method. There are those people who like to think about *Sherlock Holmes, Murder She Wrote,* or even *CSI* when they think of private detectives. There are even those within the profession who would like to see the profession not only be projected in this light but also take on some of the *CSI* characteristics. While you can unquestionably obtain that kind of expert training and therefore become more marketable to high-end clients for a number of different reasons, this is the exception rather than the rule. Fiction is best served by looking at the exception. If you have unlimited income and no time constraints, you could consider this as a viable option for the direction you want to take as a beginner. If not, then you can plan to gradually develop expertise through both formal and informal education. Of course, we don't get called out to crime scenes immediately, so the likelihood you'll find a crime scene that hasn't been altered, tainted or plain destroyed is slim to none. In working criminal defense, I have been asked to examine crime scenes, but primarily either to take pictures or to see if certain statements could be corroborated or contradicted by the physical setting. You might even have a client who believes that law enforcement missed something in their investigation, and because they are as human as anyone else, that possibility does exist. Again, the likelihood the crime scene will be as it was at the time of the incident, is slim to none. This is not to say that there will not be those occasions where a private detective might be better suited to complete an investigation than law enforcement is, but this will most often be due to legal or man-power limitations that law enforcement faces. Runaways and undercover operations at a worksite are the best example. With all this, however, it cannot be said too many times that the entry level investigator without experience, training or education, is not likely to be called upon to complete such an investigation. Undercover operations are the possible exception to that general rule.

From all these various forms of fiction, there is one rule that holds true in private investigations: **there is no such animal as useless knowledge, only knowledge that has not been properly used.** Private investigations are much more often about general knowledge, understanding people and specific knowledge related to the type of investigation to be performed and the related laws and regulations.

This is not to say that a good private detective does not prepare as much as possible by attempting to gain insightful knowledge. In fact, a phrase I first encountered in my military days has crossed over into the profession: **prior planning prevents poor performance**. And, where there is specific information available, you should learn it—for your sake, as well as the client's. Learning should be a constant in the profession, especially given that laws are perpetually changing or being newly interpreted and technological advancements can give an edge to those who are familiar with them.

A good investigator will develop his or her own procedures for ensuring that answers to certain questions are arrived at in a methodical way from investigation to investigation. Consistency will be very important to ensuring basic, and therefore important, aspects of an investigation are conducted properly and done so for each investigation. It can be relatively simple to allow the diverse nature of investigations to dictate a step away from structured procedure. While I would be the first person to admit my own dislike of formulas and procedures, improvisation and creativity have their place only *after* application of these. And, whether they would admit it or not, most private detectives embarked on their careers with the thinking that they were going to escape someone else's formulas and procedures and would always welcome thinking that was "outside the box."

This general application of the scientific method should be utilized wherever possible at every step of the investigation. The use of our knowledge, skills and experience in a methodical way will unquestionably, substantially contribute to the likelihood of the success of an investigator. But being able to think outside the box and being able to apply creative thinking and improvisational procedures to resolve investigations is another aspect of what will contribute to greater success. The types of investigations being conducted will dictate where the balance for the application of either the scientific method or thinking outside the box will apply. They should be the focus of your attention, what you are attempting to implement, and what you rely upon to provide you success.

Having said that, there is another factor that must be discussed, more so because its dismissal by most private detectives can create unrealistic expectations for those looking to enter the field and provide just the right mystique for the practicing professional. The word I am about to mention is frowned upon, spat upon, and loathed only a little more than "creativity" by most private detectives and "acting" by those who conduct undercover operations. It is a four-letter word: *luck.* Before I proceed to discuss this any further, let me emphasize something—**you never leave any aspect of any investigation to luck.** On the other hand, when a light changing favorably allows you to maintain surveillance, or arriving five minutes early because a phone call you received that was a wrong number woke you early and put you in a place to view the exchange of money and drugs on the receiving dock, to deny the influence of outside factors is as foolish as expecting their influence.

What is problematic with this dismissal of the undeniable is that it does not allow those entering the field to realistically understand the necessity of adjusting to circumstances. Certainly, if it makes you more comfortable, you could refer to these factors merely as *circumstances outside your control*, and this is actually an accurate description. But, what has been created both by fiction and by the industry is a desire to create the image of a professional who is capable of controlling every circumstance, of thinking of every possible circumstantial nuance—it's a trap for the beginning investigator. Instead, beginning investigators should know that there will be events beyond their control, sometimes affecting them negatively, sometimes positively, and it is their ability to adjust, to improvise, that will dictate their continued success. If you meet a private detective who tries to tell you that every investigation he conducted was resolved only through his skills, knowledge, planning and a strict set of procedures, you have met either a private detective who has performed a very narrow scope of investigations or a liar.

Clumsy cops, brilliant private detectives. Whether you have been exposed to the myth that police officers are simpletons compared to private detectives or that there is always an antagonistic relationship between law enforcement and the private detective, neither is an accurate portrayal. My experience, and that of most private detectives I know, is that like any other profession, law enforcement has its "bad apples" and less than gifted personnel, but most of law enforcement can be cooperative and even helpful at times. Something to keep in mind is that there are just as many "bad apples" and less than gifted personnel in the field of private investigations.

From working undercover operations to locating runaways, it has been my experience that law enforcement will afford you the same respect that is given to them. And, whether we like it or not, there simply are times when their mission carries a higher priority than ours, and their resources are much better. They have social service and counseling personnel available for the runaway, and their juvenile detectives typically have at least some training and/or education in those areas. They have access to networking with other agencies across the country and access to labs for analysis of various types of evidence. When mutual respect is the operating standard, there should be no reason for the existence of an antagonistic relationship between law enforcement and the private detective.

CHAPTER TWO

The Private Detective Defined, or How Do I Know If I'll Be a Good Investigator?

Probably one of the most frequently asked questions from people taking classes that I teach is, *how do I know if I'll be a good investigator? Or, what does it take to be a good investigator?* And, of course, there are always those people who have been told that they would make a good investigator. Someone who can specifically define a set of prerequisites to determining who will/won't be a good private detective, is someone to stay away from. There are certain qualities or characteristics common to most good investigators. There are even certain skills shared by them. But, as is demonstrated by the fact that this chapter has no strict, defined direction and reads like a continuing conversation, there is no one definitive good investigator formula, no one particular background that will ensure success. The very nature of our industry, in the sense that there are numerous types of investigations requiring different approaches, and that there are constant changes occurring in the client base, defies strict definitions.

Procedural/regulatory basics. Before going into the more subjective presentation of my thoughts and ideas, there are certain regulations in the State of Illinois that should be put forward as a matter of covering the basics. If you are reading this in another state, you can skip ahead. Again, is the index contains a list of what agency/agencies to contact in each state in that the profession is regulated. In Illinois, the current incarnation of the agency (I say this, because like so much else in government, shape-shifting does occur with new administrations) is the Department of Financial and Professional Regulation. Private detectives fall under the Division of Professional Regulation. These are the folks responsible for oversight of the licensed professionals and for amending, altering, and enforcing all the regulations contained within the Private Detective, Private Alarm, Private Security and Locksmith Act of 2004, *a/k/a* 225 ILCS 447. Because Illinois is a well-regulated state, anyone interested in entering the field needs to be aware of these regulations and requirements before proceeding further. All professions, their related acts, applications and other information can be researched and downloaded at www.idfpr.com.

The Permanent Employee Registration Card. (PERC—also commonly referred to as the blue card, because—you guessed it—it's blue in color). All employees of a licensed Private Detective Agency must have within thirty days of employment a PERC. In order to be eligible to obtain the Permanent Employee Registration Card, you must meet the following requirements:

- be 18 years of age;
- be a U.S. Citizen;
- complete a criminal background check; and,
- complete twenty hours of training.

Operational definitions. In determining the good investigator, we must first, at least to a limited degree, define the position. Operational definitions are perhaps the only realistic hope of defining the investigator in a general sense and also specific types of investigations. A good, general definition for the investigator is **a trained, professional observer, gatherer and reporter of facts.**

This defines what it is that the investigator must be capable of doing. And, while there is a tendency on the part of certain practitioners to try to say that one particular skill, for instance observational skills, communication skills, or research skills, is most important, this is impossible to strictly limit for the very same reasons. All investigations, even of the same general nature, will not necessarily be resolved through the same procedures, using the same set of skills. The following is a list of those skills that can contribute to the making of a good investigator (no one particular skill should be singled out as of priority importance; rather, each needs to be cultivated to the same degree):

- Observational skills—include listening as well as paying attention to detail during research.
- Communication skills—often referred to as "people skills," this also requires that the good investigator is a good listener. It requires the investigator to be aware of elements of both verbal and non-verbal communication and to be conscious not only of others' communication but also of his or her own in order to control the reaction of people to the investigator.
- Research skills—often overlooked, or perhaps referred to incorrectly, these skills are often what will make the investigator more than moderately successful. From the Clerk of the Circuit Courts Office to the local library, there are numerous sources for the researcher to draw from and gather information. The number of sources known to the investigator, and the degree of attention paid to detail, will determine the level of success.
- Report-writing skills—perhaps the most over-looked skill (when was the last time you saw Magnum or Jessica Fletcher writing reports?), this is often the end product on that the evaluation of our services is based. With surveillance and undercover work in particular—where the real money is being made right now—clients expect well-written reports. And, given that a good percentage of reports will make their way in front of various arbitration boards, investigating committees, or even courtrooms, it is important to try to be certain the report is well-written. This may preclude your having to appear to testify because smart defense/respondent attorneys will only want you in court if they believe your report raises doubts or could damage credibility.

These are the four primary skills for a successful investigator. They are the foundation. There are, of course, other skills that may factor into making someone successful in certain areas. Photography, fork-lift, or martial arts, are all skills that might assist in certain types of work, but they are not essential in the sense that their uses are limited. Photography can help in surveillance, supporting undercover operations, crime-scene photography, and accidents, but is of very little use to resolving a locate investigation or service of process on the average. Being able to drive a fork lift is a useful skill to have as an undercover operative in the current job market. A knowledge of martial arts can impress a client interested in executive protection, but, while useful in defending yourself always, this skill will not very often resolve a case. In private investigations you do not necessarily know that skills will or won't become important. Computer skills are now considered a must for certain areas of investigations. But, even technology-based skills and tactical-defense oriented skills will apply only to certain types of work and therefore should not be considered as a basis for functioning as a successful investigator.

Skills and *qualities/traits* are two very distinct things. Qualities, using this term admittedly in a very loose fashion, refer to a broader type of element. These are aspects of a person's personality that can play an important role in his or her life as a successful private investigator. Some of these, whether you argue nurture or nature is irrelevant, are either possessed by the person by the time they are an adult or never will be. Some, a person can be trained to obtain. The reason that certain investigation companies, for instance, will often employ persons with a military background over those without is that, especially at an entry-level, self-discipline and self-confidence are important. The military attempts to instill both of these in people, as well as the idea of paying attention to detail. The following is a list of those qualities:

- common sense
- street sense
- curiosity
- creativity
- analytical reasoning
- adaptability
- self-discipline
- self-confidence
- patience
- persistence

Common sense is quite often confused with street sense. This is demonstrated by the number of licensed private detectives who assume a college degree is indicative of a lack of common sense. Common sense is one of those intangible aspects that you either have by the time you are eighteen or never will have. It is what tells you not to drive alone at night into areas ruled over by the Gangster Disciples just to serve a Summons and Complaint on a member who is a shooter. Common sense will dictate that you don't borrow from Peter to pay Paul. Common sense can often point in the direction an investigation should take because it is common sense that dictates logical proceedings or, more accurately, proceeding in a direction as determined by the use of simple reasoning with a reference to human behavior and what people are most likely to have done. Common, or "horse", sense is an invaluable quality. Common sense would tell you that, if the job market is more favorable to those people who have a college education, a college education would be a good thing to obtain. Common sense is, however, quite different than street sense.

Street sense, or street smarts, is having knowledge of what is currently correct behavior on the "streets." It is knowledge of terminology such as "stepped on" being the newer term for "cut," as in drugs such as cocaine and heroin being diluted by additives. It is knowledge such as the idea that gang members will have an open tear-drop tattooed on when a member of their gang is killed and have the tear-drop filled in when the death has been avenged. It is knowing the current tools and method of operation for car-theft rings. It is knowing that throwing good product into the garbage to be picked out later is a common method of stealing from the company. Common sense would dictate, these are not often the things the average person is concerned with and are not a question of logical proceedings; thus, they are not common sense. And, street sense, unlike common sense, can be obtained simply by exposure. It is street sense that many degreed people sometimes lack. It is still true that a good percentage of college-educated people were not working while going through college and come from families with a substantial income. They are not exposed to certain elements or aspects of society, just as the average gang-banger would probably not know that was the salad fork. Just as a person can have book smarts and no street smarts, a person can have street smarts and no common sense, or vice-versa.

Like common sense, **curiosity** and **creativity** cannot be taught, trained, or from the outside put into a person. Curiosity is what may, hopefully with common-sense as a balance, cause a person to take the extra step to discovery of a solution. For those who don't know it, there is more to the familiar expression "curiosity killed the cat," and that is, "but satisfaction brought him back." Curiosity and creativity both need to be tempered by common sense. Creativity can get you past certain brick walls, but, when allowed to grow beyond reason, it can trap you. Hence the popularity in law enforcement, investigations and the military for the acronym K.I.S.S.—keep it simple, stupid.

Knowledge. In the beginning chapters to any work professing to inform people about private investigations, and particularly attempting to do so to train people to enter into the field, knowledge is perhaps one of the most important subjects to be addressed. Because there are so many misconceptions, it is that much more important. These misconceptions, myths, or misnomers can partially be blamed on fiction (television, Hollywood, and literary) but also on people within the industry. The cloud of mystique surrounding our industry is something a percentage of practitioners would prefer is not cleared up. It is easier, after all, to make more money if the general public perceives us as a completely unique breed of people: a group of people who are half-cop, half magician, hunting cases down with tenacity and some strange innate ability. Before starting the discourse (I'll try to make that brief) on knowledge, there are a couple of key phrases you should know. They should remain a basis of your operating philosophy—no matter what type of investigations you're conducting:

- *knowledge is power, and*
- *there is no such thing as useless knowledge; rather, there is often knowledge not put to its appropriate use.*

Knowledge, much more so than a firearm, handcuffs, or even the more practical camcorder, should be considered your most powerful tool. And, despite what any person might say about the particular knowledge you might possess or be departing to them through conversation, no knowledge is trivial in this industry. What has to be remembered is that you probably won't know ahead of time when your trivia from reading *Spiderman* and *The Fantastic Four* as a child will become important, but, if you recognize the time that it is and act upon that, it can make all the difference in the world.

With the exception of certain types of work, one of the more important parts of most investigations will be talking to people who can provide you with information. Establishing a common ground for conversation will be important. Personalizing the interview to make someone feel she is talking to a person somewhat like her will be a valuable skill. Whether it is recognizing the stuffed fish on the wall as a Musky, knowing the name of the print pattern on the wall-paper, or being able to talk about "the crib, five-o, snowbird, etc," it is unlikely that you will ever possess useless or trivial knowledge, at least in relation to getting this type of work done.

Of course, no one person can really know about everything as was suggested by Sir Arthur Conan Doyle. Nor will it often be true that forensics or related information will be of importance. But, I would not be the one to tell someone not to learn about anything, especially given the current conversations about privatization and the fact that it is extremely difficult to predict where the industry will find its next growth area. Computer forensics, accounting, and economic espionage are areas that will be growing. And, to the best of my ability, I'll be getting as much education as I can afford to because even I recognize the necessity of continuing to learn. I can't remember who I heard the phrase from, but, in this business, the day you ***stop*** learning is the day you **start** dying. Imagine trying to be an undercover operative, working day to day with people who know nothing about and care nothing about law enforcement, criminal justice, or related matters, and that's the only subject matter you're versed in. Imagine, being the tough, strong, silent type, when undercover operations require you to make contact with all different types of people. Yes, initially, you'll want to keep a little to yourself. That is what is normal for most people to do at a new job. And, ***that*** is what the undercover operative specifically, and the good investigator in general, is trying to do. Do what is normal for most of the people in that particular set of circumstances. But, when it comes time to start "cultivating" your sources at the client's company, if you have no basis for conversation, you'll get nowhere. And, despite what other people might tell you, just walking up to people and asking them if they do drugs, steal from the company, or commit other violations *is* a really bad idea. Outside of the legal issues (entrapment has been found to apply to certain civil cases), you've probably just tipped everyone off that you're five-o. Make the people comfortable with you. Talk about music, sports, XBox—whatever it is that's important to them. Become one of the "guys" or "girls." Then, they'll be the ones bringing the real areas of your concern up in conversation.

And, undercover operatives are only the most obvious example of where this applies. If you do a lot of locates or criminal investigations, these principles will apply also. In real criminal investigations, interrogations and certain types of locate investigations, knowing about that particular person's criminal, civil or even financial history often might be enough to unsettle him or her. And, under certain circumstances, knowledge is a tool to make people uneasy, just as it is to make people feel relaxed or comfortable, for instance, if you were searching for a fifteen year old runaway female. You know she has been hanging with a twenty-two year old gang-banger with previous convictions. Knowledge of his history, along with laws relating to Criminal Sexual Assault, and/or Harboring a Runaway, would be helpful in convincing him to tell you where she's at. Authoritative explanations of the law, along with assurances that the runaway *will* tell her parents and law enforcement everything (that is, actually, normally true in the case of the runaway whose behavioral patterns began to change as a result of associating with different people) can convince people to give out a little more information than they might otherwise.

Human nature should most assuredly be considered an important area of knowledge. People are not purely logical. It is very rare that you encounter someone who can afford a logical explanation for everything that they do. Nonetheless, there are some basic truths about people that need to be kept in the forefront of knowledge when trying to determine the who and why questions.

- People are creatures of habit.
- People rarely do anything for no reason.
- People engaged in criminal/illicit activity are usually driven by one of two motivators: greed or revenge.
- People like to feel important.
- People like to feel needed.
- Mama always knows (in locates).
- Blood is not always thicker than water (you'd be surprised how fast family will "drop dimes" on each other).
- Everyone has something that he or she is afraid of.

Of course, there are many more aspects of human nature. Though most people don't know it, the professional who knows more about people than any other is the successful, professional private detective. Unfortunately, in a manner similar to law enforcement, we don't always see the best side of people/human nature, that is one of the reasons it's always refreshing to work on locates related to missing children, runaways, and adoption searches.

Knowledge is like any other tool, though. To possess knowledge, even in great quantity, does not, in and of itself, guarantee success. It is the appropriate application of that knowledge that will determine a level of success. And, in any introductory text to private investigations, the *tools of the trade* have to be part of the treatment. Knowledge is perhaps the most important of those.

Tools of the trade. Like any other industry, ours is one that is affected by technological advancement to a certain degree. Computers are assisting the modern investigator not only in ensuring that reports are easier to do correctly, completely and quickly but also are becoming one of the most important tools in the newest exploding area for the private sector—computer-based white collar crime. Computer fraud, identity theft, and economic/industrial espionage have become the domain of the computer proficient. Recognized experts in the fields of terrorism/counter-terrorism and espionage are all pointing to the idea that there will soon be a new niche—the private sector, computer-based fraud and espionage investigator.

As with any other profession, cell-phones, GPS, lap-tops and other advances such as extensive databases are quickly becoming part of the standard equipment. Most offices can't operate without at least one or two information databases now. These are all types of equipment that can make certain tasks easier. And, in the future, it is very likely that more technological advancements might be cause for the elimination of some of the below-listed tools. For now though, and at least as long as electronic devices require a power source that can fail and not be quickly and easily replaced or a connection to a satellite that can experience interference or similar limitations, there will always be a good reason to become familiar with the stand-bys: pen and paper, telephone, camera (still, 35mm), camcorder, mini-recorder, binoculars, and a map-book

An operational vehicle is a basic tool also. While certain types of investigative research and background investigations could be completed using public transportation, the agency or detective doing other work besides that will need to be much more mobile.

A firearm is not, in any way shape or form, a basic or essential tool. There are certain types of work that can be performed in particular states (Illinois, for instance) under the detective license that might necessitate carrying a firearm, executive protection work being the most obvious example. Someone who feels that they want to be protected by an agency will most often want at least some of the personnel to be armed. The appropriate use of common sense, street smarts, and "people skills" should be what a professional investigator relies upon in most situations. Many people will talk about going into bad neighborhoods or being involved with drug transactions during undercover operations as reasons to carry. If the neighborhood's that bad, you'll be dead before your weapon clears the holster if someone is serious. Either bring law enforcement with you or stay out, especially if you believe carrying a firearm will save your life. And, for those macho guys who say things like, "well, I'll stand my ground, get the job done, or at least take a couple of them with me when I go," I have only two questions. Did you get into this business to be a dead hero? And, do you really believe that there's a client who pays enough to get dead for? Despite the fact the Maltese Falcon was a far departure from reality in a number of ways, it was quite accurate in its portrayal of an intelligent, street-wise, Samuel Spade who stayed away from firearms. Firearms and martial arts knowledge do have their place in the industry—a very limited place. Just as a law enforcement background being a requirement is a myth, so is the knowledge of firearms and/or martial arts. Most of the work currently being performed by successful detective agencies requires computer, note-taking, photography, video and telephone (communication) skills, and because the location of work can change from day to day, map-books (GPS) and binoculars (for rural locations or if you are riding with a partner—the passenger can watch the suspect vehicle while the driver can concentrate on driving without getting too close to the subject). The mini-recorder allows the lone surveillance investigator to take "notes" while concentrating on driving and the subject. And, though talking to one's self in the car might seem a little funny at first, think about the people who do other things while driving down the highway. A mini-recorder can also be effectively used in regards to interviews and getting direct quotes correct. Getting a person's permission, particularly where it is a distinct possibility that your report will be entered into any official record, is necessary in the State of Illinois. If you do a substantial amount of work where interviews are common, you will want to have a mini-recorder for both those occasions when you are recording for transcription of a statement later and for those occasions when you simply want to review the tape later to clarify aspects in your own mind. For instance, when performing complicated locates, you may talk to as many as six or seven people in one day. Taking notes could be cumbersome. Recording the conversations to play back later so that you can cross-reference statements and information is not a bad idea.

A brief word on pretexting. There are those professionals in the industry who recoil at the use of the word pretext, saying that they would never use a pretext to accomplish an investigation. I know a couple of these people, and I do respect their opinion. I cannot, however, subscribe to their statements, especially because, in at least one instance, I know that the person runs an agency that performs undercover operations. In undercover operations, the investigator is adopting an entire pretext identity.

A pretext is when the investigator represents herself as someone other than who she is in order to obtain information that she believes she might otherwise not be able to obtain. And, this is one of the important aspects for the investigator to remember about using a pretext—**they should be used only when the investigator can demonstrate that all other reasonable means have been exhausted, when the investigator can stipulate a reasonable belief that the person is unlikely to be honest if asked otherwise, and/or when the investigator is using the pretext not to obtain information but to determine facts relevant to the immediate status of an investigation** (for instance, a pretext phone call to the address of the subject of surveillance to determine whether or not anyone is home). **However, pretexting should not be used in attempting to effectuate service of process.**

Because there are people who have already put together complete books on pretexting, I will not attempt to dwell on this subject at great length. The nature of pretexting is such that it will often need to be adapted to the circumstances at hand, as well as the amount of information known to the investigator. And, the investigator must remember the objective of the pretext when deciding what pretext to use. For instance, with a locate, a pretext will most often be designed to elicit information.

Pretexting, or *gagging* as it is often called by people of the "old school," is often a necessary aspect of completing an assignment. If you work for different people en route to obtaining your own license, you may work for one of the people who make statements such as, "I don't pretext; I tell people who I am and why I'm there," or, "this isn't the Rockford files; we're professionals with a right to the information we're asking for." There are those people who refuse to pretext, or so they say. Imagine, if you will, attempting to get information from someone who is protecting the subject you need to locate by identifying yourself as one of the people he's trying to hide from. The odds are not good that you'll get any information. And, if someone is hiding from law enforcement or other people and wasn't aware that your client also wanted him found, chances are you may have just pushed him to run a little harder by making him feel more threatened. The idea that people *should* cooperate because you identify yourself as having a legitimate reason for wanting information is a nice idea, but then, if people always did what they should, there would be little need for us or law enforcement for that matter.

The pretexts not to use. Pretexting requires a good degree of imagination. There are certain pretexts that are commonly used and often effective that will be covered later. On the other hand, you will need to be able to innovate. Especially for the beginning investigator, however, it is important that you understand who you can't represent yourself as.

- a.) ***Law enforcement, at any level.*** In this instance, being arrested is the drawback. It is a crime, a Class 4 felony in the State of Illinois, which can result in not less than one year but not more than three years of imprisonment, to impersonate a peace officer. Generally speaking, correctional facilities are a bad place to be spending time.
- b.) ***A government representative/agent/official, at any level.*** Once again, by representing yourself in this capacity, you are, in fact, breaking the law and could find yourself paying various fines or perhaps getting a nice rest in a state-supported facility. This includes such organizations as the census bureau, the Forest Preserve District, Streets and Sanitation, etc. Basically, if it's a government (city, state, local, municipal) position, you can't be it.
- c.) ***An agent or representative of a real or existing entity.*** This is a sort of catch all that we use. Essentially, if it's an organization, association, company, corporation, fraternity (F.O.P.), union, or anything that actually exists, you can't use it as a pretext. Using package, pizza, or floral delivery as a pretext for Service of Process is acceptable, but to say you're from U.P.S., Domino's, or Amlings, could put you on the bad side of a civil lawsuit. Depending upon the states you're working in, there may also be criminal charges in relation to representing yourself as a member of a charitable organization.
- d.) ***An attorney, priest, doctor, or member of a profession wherein a reasonable person would have an expectation of privacy/confidentiality.*** An expectation that a conversation would remain confidential is related to an expectation of privacy, and in some cases, particularly in reference to attorneys and doctors, there are actually criminal penalties involved also.

Pretexting in general. Pretexting is another example of the idea that knowledge is power and that there is no such animal as useless knowledge, but there is knowledge that is not put to its appropriate use. *The more you know about an individual, the easier it will be to develop a successful pretext.* This, of course, must be balanced by your own knowledge, depending upon the purpose of the pretext. Particularly where you are attempting to obtain a fair amount of information, you have to be ready to answer questions in return. For instance, knowing that someone had served in the United States Army can provide you with the option of representing yourself as an old Army buddy who's in town for a surprise visit. Of course, if you know nothing about the Army, you could get caught by even simple questions about time spent on active duty. Your own knowledge about music, drafting, driving a forklift, or anything in general may provide the grounds to develop a pretext specific to a set of circumstances. Because you never know who you might be looking for or what circumstances will dictate your actions on an investigation, you cannot assume even trivial knowledge has no worth. Knowledge of history, for instance, might allow you to initiate a conversation supposedly based on your interest in a particular home or area. Having gotten someone comfortable in speaking with you, cleverly worded questions might not be noticed by the person you're questioning.

Some of the standard pretexts. Another factor to remember about people is that people do things for a reason; people have a *motivation* for acts and omissions of action. In the same way, they will need a motivation to give you information. In a fair percentage of circumstances, the two most common motivators for criminal activity—greed and revenge—will be the motivators to be used. Pretexting should not be considered a necessary tool for all situations or circumstances. For instances, when searching for a runaway or a missing child and with most adoption searches, a pretext is not necessary. In those cases, a majority of the population will be motivated to give whatever assistance/information they might be able to just out of common decency and respect. Yes, you will run across some people who don't want to "get involved" or people who will say things like, "sorry, it's not my problem; I've got enough of my own problems," and those people who just honestly don't know anything. But then, that is one of the real challenge of this profession: there are no always or never absolutes. Improvisation and adaptation are as perpetual as the ground rules and standard operating procedures.

- ***Pizza, package, or floral delivery.*** This will help to determine if someone is home, and hopefully get that person to the door for whatever reason. Remembering not to represent yourself as an existing company, you can use props effectively. Pizza boxes, thermal carrying bags, a single, long-stemmed rose in a box, or just the box are all props that can help move the person toward the door. Again, remember a pretext has to be believable—don't do or say anything that might betray the pretext. Also, remember that there are times when certain pretexts work best. Monday night football, for instance, leaves most football enthusiasts vulnerable. Just make the address a couple of numbers off, or ask to use the phone to call the restaurant to see what the manager wants to do about the "crank call". A fair percentage of the time, people will want the pizza even if they didn't order one.
- ***Marketing surveys.*** Intended primarily to elicit or confirm information, the risk with these is that the people legitimately don't want to answer a survey. If they will, you should have a series of questions ready with the questions you really want answered buried in between others. For instance, you are looking for someone who is behind on their child support, and you have located a sister or mother who lives in a nearby area. Design a pretext survey that allows for asking questions of both male and female members of the household. This way, even if the sister answers the phone, you will have the option of asking to speak with a male member of the household around the age of your subject.
- ***Contest winners.*** Although law enforcement in recent years has gotten much publicity for using this pretext with fugitives, this is one method borrowed from the private sector. Everybody loves free stuff. Everyone loves to win contests. And, by using the appropriate aspects of a true contest—the winner must sign for the prize and sign a release waiver for his or her name to be used in advertising—you can make people tell you where they're at.
- ***Insurance company***—You can be the investigator who is looking for witnesses to an accident that occurred somewhere in a vicinity you believe the subject may have frequented. Your company's client stands to obtain a substantial judgment. Witness fees will be provided. Playing upon the greed of people is the key here. Hopefully, they don't know what most people are given for witness fees. If they do know, hopefully they'll want to squeeze the

supposed victim of the supposed accident for more money. What is humorous is that, in a fair percentage of cases, even though these people may be trying to hide, they won't even stop to think how someone identified them as a possible witness.

- ***Personalized pretexts*** By this I mean pretexts developed in direct relation to the particular investigation and/or addressing the subject personally. Men can be the easiest targets. An attractive woman, or even just a woman with a sexy voice, can cause a man who is on the run to give directions to his doorstep. Many men assume they are desirable *and* assume a woman can pose no threat, even men who have been through "the system," or who have a criminal career. Or you could use an old army buddy in for a surprise visit or an old college friend in for a surprise visit. There are many more.

As was stated, this is only a brief word. A good investigator will have a library covering a variety of subjects. Books related to anything from medical science to Ireland to vampirism may contain information that, based on your knowledge of the subject or other persons, will prove useful. Becoming a good investigator is a learning process. Part of this will be to learn to pretext. As with the other chapters in this book, however, I am not attempting to make you an expert; instead, I am attempting to get you started in a direction toward that expertise.

Basic legal concepts. In the State of Illinois, there is no education requirement for private investigations beyond the initial twenty hours of training necessary to obtain the Permanent Employee Registration Card. It is one of the good things about the industry in a certain sense. You could, with only a high school diploma, work in the industry from age eighteen, be eligible to take the licensing exam at twenty-one, and be a licensed professional capable of earning seventy-five dollars an hour or more without any higher education. Of course, common sense would tell you that it is a good idea to obtain higher education, even if it is done along the way and without the focus necessarily being on obtaining a degree.

Criminal Justice and/or business courses should be your focus. But, short of this, you should still have an understanding of the underlying principles of the Criminal Justice system and a grasp of some of the very basic procedural aspects. Civil Code and Procedure will also be necessary to know, and I personally recommend taking a few Paralegal courses to obtain this knowledge. Of course, you can learn these things *along the way*, so to speak, but then some of it you may find yourself learning the hard way.

What I will attempt to do here is provide the basic information that will assist you in having a basic understanding and perhaps the ability to use this frame of reference for making those decisions you will have to when you are out in the field. Something to remember is that most private detective agencies are hoping to hire people they feel confident to send out in the field to accomplish tasks with minimal supervision. Hopefully, a basic understanding of some of the considerations with respect to law will assist you in being that person and therefore advancing your career.

The reasonable person standard. One of the underlying principles of most of our law is supposed to be this standard. It is simply whether or not, when determining if an act should or should not be considered a violation, a reasonable person, given this set of circumstances, would be likely to arrive at the same conclusion. For instance, in determining whether or not you may be violating a person's expectation of privacy by attempting to obtain video footage of their activities, you need to examine what a reasonable person would think is his or her expectation of privacy in that setting. If you can see that anyone walking down the street could observe the subject's activity, then you will likely not have any reason to be worried about getting the video. On the other hand, if you had to use camouflage paint, wear camouflage clothing, and climb a tree to see over someone's nine foot, solid fence, chances are you might find that your efforts are considered "extraordinary measures," and have violated a reasonable person's expectation of privacy.

Of course you might be tempted to say, well, how can anyone say what is reasonable when people are so different? This is a good point for a humorous discussion, but most judges will not see the humor if you are using that thought process to justify what you do out in the field. This basic principle is a good one to keep in mind as it addresses the common sense that should be applied to making decisions about what to do or not to do when out in the field.

Expectation of Privacy. Despite the image of the private detective as the person who can professionally violate the expectation of privacy that most people have, this is not true. While it is true that we sometimes have to develop and determine methods that are alternatives to directly addressing a problem, we are still obligated to operate not only within the boundaries of specific regulations, and criminal law and procedure but also civil code and those areas of legal principles that apply to what we are doing. Your common sense principle here should be that if most people would believe that they have an expectation of privacy in the given circumstances, you need to expect whatever you might do that would violate that expectation could eventually put you in trouble and render whatever information you obtained as useless in a legal proceeding. When working for an attorney in relation to a criminal or civil matter, you will fortunately have a client who can advise you of what they see the legal limitations are, but this will not always be the case. Remember, one of the good things about working under someone else's license, is that they are charged with the responsibility of ensuring their investigators are capable of making these decisions.

Where there is not an attorney or other person of authority to make the decision, there again think of what you or most people you know would believe their privacy rights are in that given set of circumstances. Locates present perhaps the best example. For instance, if performing an adoption search in a state where adoption records are sealed, it would probably be best to consider that the operating guideline for informing your client of what you have learned should be that you do so only after speaking with the biological parent/child/sibling whom you have located on behalf of your client. Sealed records are likely to be considered what most people believe provides them an expectation of privacy with respect to persons obtaining that information. And, having performed my fair share of adoption searches, I can comfortably say that there are legal methods of discovering that information without accessing sealed records. The fact that those records are sealed should communicate to the private detective that caution needs to be taken with the dissemination of that information.

Dissemination of information is one of the primary concerns for the private detective regarding the expectation of privacy, as well as in relation to other legal considerations. There are many different, legal methods of obtaining information, and there are very few restrictions from simply possessing information. If in the process of trying to locate you to serve you court documents I should discover your social security number, I am not in any trouble as long as my methods were within legal guidelines. If, however, I provide that number to anyone who does not have a legal necessity for that information, there are regulations that I would be violating. Because it is most often clear what is illegal when obtaining information, in this field it is more important to consider the possibilities of trouble related to dissemination of information, rather than obtaining it. This, like the consideration of whether or not to shoot that video or take that picture, needs the application of the expectation as a simple, common sense principle of what we believe most people expect.

Criminal law and procedure. There are many volumes written on criminal law and procedure, and it is not my intention to convey that you need to read them all or that you need not know any of it. For the most part, what entry level and even experienced investigators need to know about criminal law and procedure is minimal. You will want to become more versed over time if the idea of working on criminal cases intrigues you, and, for those practicing in the State of Illinois, you will need to know criminal law and procedure to pass the private detective exam. The most important basic concepts that every investigator should have an understanding of with respect to criminal law and procedure are the following elements of a criminal offence. There are others that relate to certain types of investigations, but I will address those in those chapters.

Elements of a criminal offense. For every criminal offense, except possession offenses, there are two elements that need to be present and proven by the prosecutor in order for a conviction—well, in theory anyway.

- *Actus Reus*: an act or behavior. Of the two elements, this is typically the easier one for a prosecutor to show. Either the act or behavior related to the offense (property was taken, a battery occurred, etc.) happened, or it did not. The second element, on the other hand, is not quite so obvious.
- *Mens Rea*: the accompanying mental state. Each criminal act, crimes of possession again being the exception, has a mental state that is stipulated within that statute, and also needs to be proven in order for a conviction to be found. For instance, if someone took your MP-3 player from your car, in order to show a conviction for theft from the auto, a prosecutor would need to be able to show that it was taken with *the intent to permanently deprive the owner of the use or benefit of.* So—and this is a stretch—a person could say in his defense that he was only going to borrow the device while he went for a run, and then would have returned it. If the prosecutor could not prove otherwise, there should not necessarily be a conviction in this matter.

The four mental states are *intent, recklessness, negligence and knowledge*. While intent is typically associated with the most serious crimes, it should be noted that what is most important for the investigator to know is the mental state that is associated with the specific criminal act that they may be investigating or that they otherwise have reason to possess knowledge of in their activities.

The Criminal Justice System. A basic understanding of the mechanics of the Criminal Justice System should be something that most investigators possess as well. Though you might rarely have reason to utilize this knowledge while completing your day to day assignments, completing them with minimal difficulty can be assisted by having this knowledge.

Complaint-based system. What every investigator should be aware of is that our Criminal Justice System is initiated by a complaint that law enforcement responds to. In simple terms, what this means for the investigator is that the more inclined you are to be confrontational or hostile with people, the more likely you are to have to become familiar with the further workings of the system. The best example of what I mean by this is demonstrated in a brief story of what happened to one investigator. In attempting to interview a subject about the location of certain property, which that subject was in possession of in violation of a contractual agreement, the investigator chose to respond to the subject's confrontational nature with a similar response. Not only did this not result in information, but after the investigator left, the subject called local law enforcement and reported the investigator's behavior with some exaggeration. Law enforcement, knowing only what they had been told by one of their citizens, responded and intercepted the investigator as he was departing the area. The investigator was arrested on aggravated assault charges because the subject had complained that the investigator threatened the use of force while displaying hand-cuffs in a threatening manner. That was not what had happened, and the subject declined to go to the police station to sign a formal complaint. The subject, however, had accomplished his objective. The investigator had ruined his day, and he had caused the investigator to have a difficult day. Some would say the investigator should have pursued a complaint against the subject for filing a false report, but the truth is that the subject was easily able to say he was "shaken up" by the incident but had decided it was not worth someone going to jail.

I am not attempting by this example to say that an investigator should not be direct, authoritative, or otherwise attempt to communicate that they will not be deterred by the confrontational nature of a subject. Rather, I am hoping to impart that common sense should dictate to what degree any particular circumstance requires a balance of standing firm and appearing to be more cooperative with the subject. You will learn over time to determine if a subject might actually be talked into being cooperative if they have a sense that you are not "out for blood." I have had more than one experience when my appearance of being sympathetic with a subject resulted in that subject providing me the information that I sought. And, given that the client was paying to have that information obtained, the choice was correct.

CHAPTER THREE

Service (of Process) with a Smile

Service of process is often treated the same way that domestic surveillance investigations are treated by many of the *hard-boiled, high profile, real-tough-guy* private detectives: they don't have the time for it, and it's not real work for a real detective. The fact is that there is money to be made in service of process, just as there is in domestic (infidelity) work. The number of detectives who say they don't handle domestic cases or won't do service of process is better for those who do or will. And, no matter what anyone might say, service of process is **not** simply being someone's delivery boy. In fact, service of process is probably one of the best areas to start an entry-level investigator in because it will require the development of a number of related skills. If a person can be effective performing service of process with the challenges it can present, chances are he or she will do well in other areas also.

Service of process is **the means by which a court obtains jurisdiction over a person in regards to an action at that court.** In other words, if the person is not served, he is not legally obligated to appear or file a response. Therefore, no matter how many times you tell me we have a court date, in the eyes of the court I have not been officially informed unless I have been served. Most of the legal definitions appearing in this text are drawn from the State of Illinois Code of Civil Procedure. While there may be certain differences regarding technical aspects, such as what types of service can be effected through abode service, for the most part, methods of operation will be the same from state to state. In the State of Illinois, the private detective is specifically enumerated within the Illinois Compiled Statutes as one of those people capable of effecting service of process (along with the Sheriff, his deputies, and the county coroner—Quincy, process server). In all counties with a population of less than one million (except Cook, as of this writing), this can be done without special appointment. This is also true elsewhere, though not necessarily everywhere.

A point that needs to be emphasized to the entry-level investigator, and sometimes reinforced to some veteran investigators, is that service of process involves the service of official court documents. Therefore, when you sign that affidavit that must be notarized, you are signing as if you are under oath. And, should you decide at some point, for one reason or another, to falsify an affidavit, you are subject to the criminal charge of **perjury**, as well as whatever other actions might be taken against you if you're caught. Anyone who has been in this business for a while will tell you this is a word-of-mouth, credibility-based business. Word will get around quickly if you're convicted of perjury. In the State of Illinois, the office of the State's Attorney would pursue the perjury issue. If convicted, the State's Attorney's office is obligated to inform the Department of Professional Regulation, who can then take their own action. Other states may not take this matter as seriously as the State of Illinois does. Falsification of reports or affidavits, operating without a license, charging clients for work that was never performed, firearms irresponsibility, and confidentiality seem to rank highest on the list of concerns for the Department of Professional Regulation in the State of Illinois. Especially for those readers at an entry-level, get to know the personnel at the equivalent of D.P.R. in your state now; it can only serve to help you in the long run.

Types of documents (generally). For the most part, from state to state, the types of paperwork will remain the same. The specific regulations regarding certain aspects of effective service of process of those papers may vary. For instance, in Illinois a Summons and Complaint may be served no later than thirty days after the date of issue or must be served at least seventy-two hours prior to the court date, depending upon whichever applies to that particular Summons and Complaint. A Rule to Show Cause may be served up to twenty-four hours before the court date. A Citation to Discover Assets must be served no later than five days prior to the court date. Check your own state's regulations, and remember, when serving papers from another jurisdiction, it is the rules of the jurisdiction in which the action is brought that apply.

Summons and Complaint/Petition: There must **always** be a complaint or petition accompanying the summons. The Summons and Complaint or Petition is the initiation of any action at court and is what initially will bring the parties to the action under the jurisdiction of the court. The Summons is the document that notifies the person you are serving either of the action or of when the initial court date will be for the action. In most cases, the person you are going to serve will be expecting to be served, and in some cases, divorce for instance, the person may actually be glad to see you.

Subpoena: This is the paper that requires a person who **is not** a party to the action at court to make or file an appearance. Subpoenas can be for different specifications, such as an actual court appearance, a deposition or others. Subpoenas are served to witnesses or persons who are considered sources of information relevant to the action at court, hence the term hostile witness, meaning either someone your side would rather not have testify or someone who has their own reasons not to want to testify (these can range from personal involvement with one of the parties involved to fear of retaliation from one of the parties involved).

Citation to Discover Assets: This paper requires the person named to produce various financial records ranging from wage statements to tax records to real estate holdings to company records. This type of paper will most often be issued after some decision has been reach in re the action at court, and the court wants to determine what assets one party to the action has so as to satisfy a judgment.

Rule to Show Cause: This is a written opinion of the court issued in relation to a decision made *ex parte* (with only one party present). Essentially, this paper is informing the person to be served that because they failed to appear or failed to obey an earlier order of the court, unless they appear at the listed court date, the decision made at the court date they missed will go into full force and effect. The next court date is their last chance, short of appeal, to convince the judge not to make them pay. Normally, this will mean the person to be served may be attempting to avoid service or simply has moved and is trying to ignore the entire issue. It can make these difficult to serve right away. On the other hand, a fair percentage of the time, once you find the person, they can be easy to serve if you explain the nature of the paper to them.

Order (of Protection, Temporary Restraining): These are often the most complicated form of serve in the sense that they are the most volatile. Because these orders are often in relation to domestic matters of a serious nature, the person to be served is not going to be happy to see you. A good percentage of the time you will be serving papers that inform a person that they have a few hours to pack up their belongings and vacate a residence they have occupied for a number of years, and that they must stay a certain distance from their home, children or other family. Sometimes, they will be less serious in nature. Not often enough, however. Fortunately, most police departments will be more than happy to send a unit with you to ensure that a civil disturbance doesn't result. They'd rather do that than respond to the address ten minutes later while the process server and the subject are fighting.

These are only the most common types of paperwork you will be serving. There are others, such as Wage Garnishments. There is no real *average* in regards to which papers are easiest. Wage Garnishments are most often the easiest, but whether or not you serve those will depend on what type of clients the attorneys you work for have.

Types of Service: Service of process can be effected in more than two ways, but we will focus on the two that we would be asked to perform. An attorney can effect service by mail or even publication in certain circumstances and with certain types of matters. But even where they can, they may choose not to effect service in this manner. If they are exercising any of the other options, there will be no need for them to contact your office.

Personal service:. This is the phrase that refers to serving the individual to whom the papers are directed. Personal service is not always required, but in most cases you will want to check with your boss/supervisor before you attempt service another way.

Abode Service: Abode, or substitute, service in the State of Illinois can be effected upon a person over the age of 13 who resides at the usual place of abode as the person named in the process. This can only be done at the address and requires that you explain what is required of the person named in the process. A good rule of thumb is, despite what the state allows, try not to effect abode service to anyone under fifteen. Not all types of service of process can be served abode. The two best resources for determining your area's particular requirements and restrictions are Civil Code and Procedure, and your client or someone at your client's office. It is seldom that attorneys will have reason to know the statutes regarding effective service of process, but they will know the idiosyncrasies of the judge overseeing the matter. As a general rule, at most law offices, paralegals or secretaries will often be more familiar with certain aspects of procedure and may be your point of contact.

Some General Rules: As with every other type of work that can be done in our profession, there are some ground rules. Service of process can be incredibly easy at times, and unbelievably difficult at others. Because of this frequent and wide variation, it is important to remember some basic principles.

Where a person can be served. In the State of Illinois, one of the interesting aspects of the effective service of process is that there is only one place where a person cannot be served. Yes, you can serve a person who is in jail. Yes, you can serve a person at the grocery store, movie theater or restaurant. Serving people at certain times/places—weddings, funerals, etc.—does need to have discretionary common sense applied. While it might be expedient to serve someone at his or her wedding, in most cases this would probably not be considered a good choice. Funerals, similarly, are not the best choice for a time and place to serve someone. If the person to be served is at his or her favorite tavern and has had a few or in a hospital and under any form of anesthesia, effecting service of process would be a bad choice. It could easily be argued that the person was not capable at that time of understanding the nature of what you explained to them. What is the one place you cannot serve a person? In the courtroom when a person is there as a party to an action. From a speeding ticket on up, if the person to be served is in the courtroom at the direction of the court, they cannot be served in relation to another matter. It is best to apply the rule as if it applied to the courthouse in general because certain judges view the subject's presence even in the courthouse as an aspect of the order that brought the person there. Outside the courthouse is best.

There is no black and white with service of process. As much as I think it is important to know and understand each state's service of process, I would also be the first person to tell you that you should not make decisions about what to do in a given set of circumstances based solely on them. The truth is that different judges have different views about the relative importance of any given guidelines. Your attorney clients will most likely know the judges in the circuits in that they litigate. For the most part, they would rather have you ask them questions ahead of time than listen to a lecture from a judge about a discrepancy the judge has with your service. Yes, you are responsible for knowing and following the legal procedures, but judges are capable of *interpreting* anything in law.

Read the papers you are about to serve. No, not to get a laugh at someone else's expense. Read the papers so that you know what the general nature of the action at court is; often, it's a good indicator of the likelihood you'll experience difficulty. Read to try to determine as much about the person to be served as you can. Quite often within the complaint or other paperwork there will be some information to help you determine if the person to be served is likely to be hostile or has a past history of violence. Even though I have never been shot, stabbed, or even punched, you have to remember that some people operate on the age old philosophy "kill the messenger."

Approach the person to be served on a first-name basis. This rule obviously will have some exceptions, but, for the most part, you'll want to ask for people by their first name to appear more personally associated with the individual. And, when you're meeting the person you're going to serve for the first time, asking for him by his full name, if he wants to avoid service, is a tip off that you're not an old friend or a friend of a friend. Again, common sense. How often do you feel relaxed when someone at your door asks, "Are you Mr. Jonathon C. Doe?"

Never assume your client's information is correct. Before heading out of the office, perform some basic checks like calling information, checking Reverse Directory if it's available in your area (for the Chicago area, this is now through 411, and can also be found on the internet), and calling the local library to ask the reference desk to perform a criss-cross index search. While it is true that these will not always work to provide information, especially with service of process, you will at least have information to attempt to verify. A client's information may be old, or numbers might be transposed. Save yourself a drive to find out that the person moved.

Postal forwardings are one of your best checks, and they can be done through the mail. Private detectives, attorneys, or others requiring postal forwarding, or post office box-holder information in relation to service of process, can obtain that information through the post office by filling out a form and providing the requested information. Obviously, if there is a rush situation, you will not want to wait the three to five days it might take to get back to you through the mail. But, if you go out to a location, and the people at the address say that your subject moved out, you can go to the local post office and get the forwarding information at that time, if any was left.

Never second-guess yourself in the field, but always evaluate afterwards. Like a couple of the other rules that you will see repeated in other chapters, this is one that applies to doing almost any kind of investigative work. When performing service of process, you will have to make certain judgment calls. If you have been given proper training and have made the effort to learn as much as you can, you should find that your judgment calls should be acted upon. Yes, you will make mistakes. Despite the image many practitioners put forth of never having made mistakes, everyone makes them. But, in the field, hesitation is a mistake, second-guessing is a mistake—it will only serve to complicate any error you might have made by proceeding. Evaluation afterwards is *always a possibility and should always be done so that the next time you'll know what might be a little easier.*

Coordination and cooperation with law enforcement should be regular. Despite the fact that a majority of your serves may not require that you stop and check in with law enforcement, some will. Orders of Protection, for instance, will frequently require the assistance of law enforcement. Again, if the complaint in the service of a "simple" Summons and Complaint indicates a belligerent personality, stop in and let the local p.d. know who you are, where you're going, and what you're doing. This way, if an incident does occur, you've already established the fact you've got respect for law enforcement. One thing to keep in mind about the way that law enforcement has to operate: if a citizen calls and tells them you broke into her house, were brandishing a weapon, and physically abused her while representing yourself as a Federal Agent, then they have to respond as if that was what happened. You, of course, did none of those things and weren't even in possession of a firearm. Nonetheless, if the caller/complainant is willing to press charges, you *will* be processed and have to go through the procedures of court. Granted, the complainant will probably never actually show up at court, but you'll have to. And he or she will be laughing. And, some of those belligerent people are wise-guys. So, check in when it looks like there's a potential for an incident. And, no matter what anyone tells you, most law enforcement personnel will give you the respect you show them. They are good friends to have because quite often they will be the only form of back-up available.

Document each attempt you make to effect service. Your client has the right to know that you are making some effort to effect service of process. Your client will also know that you will be assisting his efforts by establishing due diligence to serve the defendant/respondent. Though not often prosecuted, there are civil contempt charges related to those people who attempt to avoid service of process, and even for those people who interfere (friends who hide the subject, etc.) with service of process. And with service of process, there is the likelihood that you may have to perform skip-trace/locate operations in order to effect service of process on the named subject, so taking down vehicle license plate numbers as well as other notes might prove useful in that event. **Always** contact the client to obtain permission to proceed with skip-trace/locate procedures, for you will bill for this in addition to your rates for the service of process itself.

Become familiar with your State's laws/regulations regarding effect of service of process. In the State of Illinois, personal service requires only that you positively identify the person named to be served and explain the nature of the paperwork to the individual. The courts have found that it is not necessary to have the person take the papers nor to have the papers touch the person. *Don't go around throwing papers at people*—it could put you in a bit of trouble. Throwing papers at people can be construed as a hostile or provoking gesture, which could lead to a civil disturbance, which could lead to more headaches than you need. Primarily, you should be concerned with the positive identification and your attempt to explain the papers to the person. When a door gets slammed in your face or someone tries to drive away, affix the papers to a secure area and explain that in your affidavit or an attached report.

Service of process can be a stepping stone to other work. While it is true that in order to make substantial monies from performing service of process you need a high volume, other things are also true. Like, your clients for service of process will almost always be attorneys. These are the people who can provide you with a lot of other work if you prove yourself capable and make them aware of your ability to conduct surveillances, take witness statements, locate witnesses or other people, locate information, prepare backgrounds, or other services one of their clients might need.

With a Smile.
The subject to be served. Most of the people you will be serving papers to are not going to be delighted to meet you. Some of them may be courteous, polite or even friendly once in a while. A fair percentage of the time people will say little or nothing. Some of them will deliver colorful descriptions of you, your mother, your sister, and your client. A very few will threaten you with bodily harm. There are a few important things to remember. No one is paying you to get punched, stabbed or shot. No matter how fast or tough you are, there's always somebody better. Walking away is usually the best option to exercise when someone is being belligerent. Each time you engage in a physical contest, you run the risk of: raising your insurance costs; giving your own attorney more of the money to represent you that you're earning for doing that serve, making the attorney who is your client wonder if he shouldn't find another detective who can do the work without putting *him* in civil lawsuit jeopardy; and putting more money in your physician's pocket. Most of the time, even if you can't hand the person the paper, you'll still be able to effect service of process one way or the other without having to *stand your ground and get the job done no matter what.* And, as long as the serve is acceptable to the courts, you have the last laugh. There are no "always" statements in this line of work, and none of this is meant to convey the idea that you should willingly accept abusiveness. But, generally, people who actually will hurt you are not going to threaten you first; they'll just do it. In that case, so as not to be misleading, defend yourself. Verbal abuse you should learn to take as a matter of fact. Diffusing hostilities should be the objective, departing the area the alternative. Escalating hostilities by yelling back, or *not taking shit from anyone,* is for those people interested in losing their licenses, losing their savings, and possibly losing their lives. Ask yourself

one simple question: is it really important what the person you just served says or thinks about your or any member of your family?

The client. Service with a smile is just as important in this area. There will be plenty of occasions when you will want to yell. Grin and bear it. Attorneys are not detectives. Most do not think like detectives. And, in all fairness, often times what may appear to be an attorney's mistake will actually be the attorney's client's mistake. As was stated earlier, service of process on a serve by serve basis is not great money. On a volume basis, it can be. Some important things to remember that will help you retain clients and perhaps even get clients who are dissatisfied with the detective agency they're using.

- *Report to your client on progress with every serve on a regular basis.* Your client's client will want updates. Your client should not have to be stalling his client because he hasn't heard from you.
- *Get the process server's return (affidavit) back to your client as soon as possible.* Your client has to file the return with the court in order for the subject who was served to be held accountable for not showing up.
- *No matter how small the amount of work you get from an attorney, remember that, as in any business, a continuing client is a continuing client.* An occasional serve from an attorney will not make you a great deal of money. But, each client has certain needs. And, each client that you provide complete, confidential, and professional services to at a reasonable rate is a salesperson/advertisement for you. Attorneys do talk to each other about who they're using. Even if the attorney you've done work for never needs surveillance work or locate work done, there is a good chance someone he knows will.
- *Always ensure that your clients do know what other services you can provide.* It is **not** safe to assume a client will automatically regard you as someone capable of doing all types of work just because you have a license. Whether you use a newsletter, stop in and talk to the client, or merely talk to the person you normally have contact with at the client's office, let them know. If you don't, they might ask another attorney, "Who do you use to do your locate and surveillance work?"

CASE FILES: A Simple Serve

Especially as an instructor in private investigations, I am often presented with misconceptions about various aspects of the profession. The classes that I teach are introductory level in accordance with the regulations in the State of Illinois, and so most of the students have little knowledge or exposure to the reality of the industry. Like most of the general public, their knowledge of the field is limited to fiction in various media, and they are surprised to learn that there is such a publication as *PI Magazine.*

Service of process is one of those areas that has been presented in a certain light. In the case of service of process, this not only because of the fiction but also because certain practitioners have their own opinion of this type of work. Some of the fiction presents an image of constant danger; that is far from the truth. Some practitioners refer to *serving papers* (how it's commonly referred to in the field) as being nothing more than a delivery service. While it is true that at times it can be as simple as driving to an address and giving a cooperative person his or her documents, the idea that this will be the case the majority of times is accurate only if you are serving a limited type of papers to a limited type of client. One of the reasons service of process can be a good place to have an entry level investigator, as you will see, is that it can be a very good way to develop useful skills.

. . . .

"As a general rule," Tim explained, "attorneys make it a practice not to sue clients for unpaid fees. It's just bad for business."

"I could see where that wouldn't look good," I replied and took the file Tim handed me. Tim and the firm he worked for had been a client for almost seven years, and I knew we had never chased down anyone on their behalf for money that was owed. One of his partners had asked for a recommendation on a collections agency. I explained that when a private detective has to hire a collections agency, there's a bigger problem than money owed. "But this young man has pushed the limits?"

"To put it succinctly, yes. In fact, this is more about personal satisfaction than the money, so budget is *not* the first consideration here."

"Good money after bad?" I asked Tim. Because he had been a reliable client, I wanted to make sure he had thought about what he was asking.

"It'll be worth it."

"You're the boss," I answered and stood up. "I'll keep you updated."

I went back to the office and read over the file. Drake Caldwell had hired Tim in relation to a DUI charge. Tim had managed to get him off with six months of supervision, and during the course of the proceedings, Drake had moved and left no forwarding address. Tim had mentioned that he thought Drake had some kind of warrant out of DuPage County, but he wasn't sure what it was for and whether or not it was still active. Of course, one of the better aspects of working for attorneys is that typically they have more information than most clients. And on their clients they had a full information sheet, so I had name, date of birth, social security number, last known address and place of employment. Of course, I suspected that anyone who would scam his attorney might be providing less than useful information.

I had one of the investigators do the database work on Drake. No surprises. No current address, no vehicles in his name, no real property, a divorce six years ago, and at the ripe old age of twenty-three he already had two bankruptcies under his belt. He was twenty-seven now and apparently hadn't changed course much. He did have an active warrant out of DeKalb County, but nothing had shown up out of DuPage.

"You want DuPage or DeKalb?" I asked Dannielle.

"You're the boss," she answered, a grin showing at the corners of her mouth.

Dannielle had worked at the agency for a little over a year and had proved particularly useful with difficult locate investigations. It wasn't her degree in Criminal Justice or even the familiarity she had with the criminal justice system through her police officer fiancé but rather her understanding of street-level psychology that had proven useful. She, in fact, had coined that phrase. Having minored in Psychology, she often pointed out that much of the formal theory made fancy explanations of human behavior and motivations. She enjoyed repeating some of my favorite phrases.

"You're right," I said and grinned right back. "I'll take DeKalb."

The grin was because Dannielle often mentioned that she liked doing the work we had in DeKalb because it put her back where she had gone to school. I had actually chosen DeKalb because I knew law enforcement preferred to speak with the person who held the license when they were providing information. They knew that a private detective had to do some work to earn the license, but getting a PERC card to be an investigator working for an agency wasn't particularly difficult. I told Rita, our secretary, where we were going, and we both headed out.

. . . .

"So, what do we know?" I asked Dannielle, sitting down at my desk and taking a sip of coffee.

"Not much," she answered, rubbing the sleep out of her eyes.

"Still a bright and cheery morning person, eh?"

"Oh, always. It's a writ out of child support. Five and half years worth of not paying—twenty-two thousand. Guess what? Self-employed at the time and no new information."

"Shocker," I replied.

A writ of body attachment wasn't exactly a warrant, but it worked the same way. It was an order from the court directing law enforcement to arrest the person and bring him or her before a judge. The judge would then determine how much of the money owed the person would have to produce to be released with a pending court date. As much as it had elements of debtors prisons to it, it typically was only issued when a person was already in violation of a court order to make payments.

DeKalb had not proved very useful either. Although their information was more up to date, it didn't provide any answers. But, they did have names of a couple of Drake's associates and suspected the business was a sham. They had been told by everyone they had interviewed that Drake was no longer associated with the business and had moved out of state. You didn't have to be a genius to know that whatever Drake's associates might tell law enforcement was likely to be less than reliable information.

Since DeKalb had been his most recent haunt, we knew that would be where we were headed. Before we left, I made a pretext phone call to the home improvement company. It was answered by a voicemail, and I left a message about needing some paint and gutter work done. I left them the 815 blind line number. The blind line was a line that had an extra security level so that there was no way to get information for anyone but law enforcement, and we left the standard phone company voicemail greeting so no one could determine if they were calling a home or business. We had one that used a 312 area code and one that used an 815 area code. Everyone in the office knew not to answer those lines.

Not surprisingly, no one we talked to at any of the DeKalb addresses knew anything about where Drake might be, even though we spoke to half of them using the pretext of being people who knew him from hanging out at the Cotton Club. His warrant out of DeKalb was drug related, and the Cotton Club was known for being a place to hang out if you wanted to hook up. One woman and two landlords, whom we had spoken plainly with, asked if we would update them if we got any current information. While it would have been tempting to let the woman know, the landlords' attorney would be the only people we could pass any information to.

We were sitting at Kings and Queens Gyros when Rita called. Someone had called on the blind line and left a different number than the company number. We had gone to the "address" of the company. It was an answering service. Rita had gotten an address from the number, and we now had some useful information to work with. The address was in neighboring Sycamore and was listed to a Mr. and Mrs. with the same last name as one of Drake's "known associates." Danni and I both suspected he had been forced to retreat back to his parent's home. The only question was how to proceed in speaking with him.

By the time we arrived at the single family dwelling, we had determined that the best way to approach would be by properly identifying ourselves. Although he would not want to cooperate, there would be the pressure of his parents to stay out of trouble. It was very rare to find parents that honestly didn't care if their children were putting themselves in jeopardy, no matter what explanation they might provide about how their friend was being "unjustly" pursued. Fortunately, there were two newer cars in the drive, in front of the utility van with ladders atop.

"Mrs. Jenkins?" I asked the fifty-something looking woman who answered the door.

"Yes, may I help you?"

"Hello," I said, showing her my license, Danni presenting her agency identification.

"We were wondering if Brian was home?"

"Well . . . yes, he's home. He's not in any kind of trouble is he?"

"Ma'am," I answered, adding my best Joe-Friday monotone voice. "All I can really say is that we're not aware of any trouble that he's in, but he may have some information about someone else."

"It's that Drake character, isn't it?"

"Ma'am," Danni said, looking concerned and sympathetic. "We understand your concern as a mother, but really all we can say is that we hope Brian will be able and willing to help."

"If he wants any more home-cooked meals he will," she said angrily and stepped back into the house. She yelled for her son, her voice louder than her frame would have suggested was possible.

A few seconds later, after muffled and tense words between them, Brian stepped out onto the front porch. He was heavyset, tattooed and pierced in various places. While there was no such animal as definitively revealing characteristics, given what we already knew, his appearance was a good indicator that Brian was not likely to have a lot of room to maneuver.

"If this is about Drake," he said without introduction, "I don't know where he's at."

"Maybe not," Danni said, "but if you thought it was about him, you know he's only a little shy of taking people down with him."

"No way. Drake wouldn't drop dime on anybody."

"Honorable guy?" I said. "That's good. Then you should have no worries talking to us. Besides, we're not law enforcement. We can't arrest anybody."

I had told Brian the truth. In Illinois, a private detective had no more arrest authority than a private citizen, except in very rare cases when he or she was specifically named on a warrant. But, what I didn't volunteer was that, under Illinois regulations, private detectives were required to report criminal activity they became aware of in the performance of their duties. It was a calculated risk that Brian wouldn't assume we'd inform law enforcement of anything he might tell us.

"Yeah, then why are you looking for him?"

"We can't tell you who our clients are," Danni answered truthfully, "but we're only looking for him about some money he owes people."

"You guys do that? Pretty lame. I thought you guys were like CSI and stuff."

"Only in the movies and on TV."

"So, you guys won't, like, tell anyone where you got any information from?"

"Brian," I said, honestly stating a principle I believed in, "whatever you might tell us, we wouldn't volunteer to anybody. Helps us too. You know, the big mystery of where we get our information."

Brian was quiet for a minute. He looked around, back into the house, and took out a cigarette. Seeing the Natural American Spirit pack, I took mine out too. Little things, like smoking the same brand of cigarettes, allowed people to assume certain things about you. Along with my earring, the cigarettes might have helped to relax Brian a little.

Okay. Okay, I'm being straight with you though—I don't know where Drake is staying. All I got is a phone number, and he says not to call him there."

"Hey, all we're asking is you tell us what you can. If that's all you got, we go away."

He took a deep inhale and dropped the cigarette to the ground. He went back into the house, and we could hear his mother walking with him and asking him questions. We couldn't help but smile. It was a scene everyone who'd been a teenager knew, even if not for the same type of circumstances. A few seconds later, Brain came out and handed Danni a slip of paper with a phone number on it. We assured him no one would knew where we got it from, and headed back to the office.

. . . .

After trying unsuccessfully to use database information to determine the origin of the phone number that Brian had given us, Danni and I discussed how to proceed. The difficulty was that if Drake answered the phone he'd be on guard. If it was someone else, leaving a message would be tricky because depending upon his relationship to that someone else, the message would need to be modified. We agreed that if it was anyone other than Drake, calling back would be the best solution.

"Like, oh my God," Danni added, bouncing her head back and forth and flipping her long, curly blond hair with her hand. Despite the fact she was anything but the stereotypical young party girl from the suburbs, Danni did look the part, and over the telephone it only took a little modification in speech patterns. Talking faster, a little more high-pitched, and not really paying attention to what the other person was saying, Danni could disarm most young men.

I nodded. In speaking to people at various locations, it had become clear that Drake was, or at least had been, quite the lady's man. People were creatures of habit, and that old cliché didn't merely refer to where someone went to get their favorite cup of coffee or Margarita. Especially if you weren't aware of or couldn't control your weaknesses, they could be used against you. I sat back, closed my eyes and listened as Danni dialed.

"Hello? . . . Hello, Drake? . . . Oh my God, how are you? . . . Oh, I'm sure . . . . Look, I just got back in from New York, and, well, I'm still the same Rachel . . . Yes, Rachel. The Cotton Club, marketing major, sunny-side up Rachel . . . Look, I don't want to just sit here, and I can't sleep. So, like, what are you doing? I know you're up for a pitcher of Margaritas. Then, maybe, who knows? . . . For sure. I even have an expense account. You're a potential client . . . No, totally. I'm serious. Got this great rental . . . Half hour. Give me directions. I'm at the Marriott, Schaumburg . . . Good direction Drake. It's been a couple of years. Where? . . . Streamwood. Where's that? . . . Wow, wow, slow down. I don't want to wind up in some, like, whole other suburb."

Drake gave Danni directions right to the front door.

. . . .

When Drake opened the door to the elegant, split-level brick home, he didn't expect to see the Streamwood police detectives. As they were finishing advising him or his rights, I walked up and placed the summons under his arm. After the officer had finished, I explained who I was and what the papers required Drake to do. *Yeah, right* was his only response.

As I was walking out, one of the most memorable moments of my career occurred as Drake's father, dressed in an expensive-looking bathrobe, stepped out onto the landing of the stairs to the second level. He looked down, surveyed the scene, and shook his head.

"I'm gonna send you cops a bill for carpet cleaning—look at the mud."

After he said that, he turned around and walked back into his bedroom. Apparently Drake's father was all too familiar with what his son's excesses had brought to him. I could not remember having ever seen a parent so resolved in his child's fate, and I can't say that I've encountered anything quite like that since.

I tell my students this story to illustrate two things: the first is that while some services of process might occur as if you were just making a delivery, don't let anyone tell you that service of process as a rule is simple; the second is that there are limitations to technology, and private investigations will always be about working with people, pretext or otherwise. While certain investigations will be greatly altered by advances in technology, at the heart of solving the simple serve to the most complex investigation is the necessity of recognizing that ultimately some things never change.

CHAPTER FOUR

Locate Investigations

As I had forewarned, there will be times when information is repeated within this text, partially due to the idea that each type of investigation needs to have a separate and distinct treatment, devoid of reference to the previous, and partially due to the fact that anyone at an entry-level position should have certain things repeated to him or her. **No matter what you might read or hear, there are no experts in this industry.** While I cannot fault people for being shrewd business people and using the expert title that others have placed on them, the truth is that this industry does operate in a state of perpetual change based not only on law but also on technology. As regards locates, the authors have all been very successful. Are any of us experts? Specialists, yes; experts, no. The *Freedom of Information Act of 1974,* like other laws, is subject to interpretation on a regular basis. What was "public access information" last year may not be this year. Another reason that there are no experts, at the very least in relation to locates and undercovers, is that there is no way to know what knowledge you possess may be useful in resolving the case. And, no matter what anyone might say, **there is no one who can offer a guarantee.** With extensive experience in the private sector, the Army's Military Police AWOL Apprehension Section, and law enforcement to draw upon, I do not offer anyone a guarantee of success; I offer only a guarantee of my best effort and reasonable rates.

Types of Locate Investigations for the Private Detective.
Adoption searches. These can be very personally rewarding to complete. They can also be very difficult to complete. It is the type of work that leads some people to cross that line to save themselves

headaches and try to corner a market. There is a woman who is an outstanding example of why you don't break the law, especially as a private detective. She had a better rate at solving adoption searches for the volume she was doing than anyone I've ever known. I've done quite a few over a period of time with the same success rate, but not nearly as many as she did in a short span of time. Her success rate was one hundred percent. She would pay her secret. friends at the county clerk's office to open sealed adoption records, a flagrant violation of people's expectation of privacy. She's currently about half way through a one and one half year sentence at a Federal penitentiary. My method may take a little longer and cost the client a small percentage more, but I still get the job done without taking that kind of risk. With adoption searches in particular, you should be prepared to talk to a lot of people. If luck is with you—**or, should I say, if you meet with favorable circumstances and are clever enough to recognize and capitalize on them**—your client has adoptive parents who are cooperative with the search. If this is the case, you will most often have a great deal more legitimate information to start with. Something to remember about the successful adoption search. You should recommend to all your clients in this and similar circumstances that it is a good idea for all family members to think about counseling. Depending upon the circumstances, the emotional impact of any adoption search can be profound. You will probably find that bringing siblings together is almost always a happy occasion, whereas bringing your client together with biological parents, or parents and siblings, can create emotional upheavals.

"Friendly" and/or "Family" Locates. These particular types of locate investigations need to be given scrutiny. No matter how much cash a prospective client may lay on the table in front of you with the promise of more upon successful location of his or her "friend" or "family" member, you should exercise certain precautions to protect yourself from becoming involved in a wrongful death lawsuit. *Inform your prospective client that you cannot reveal to him the address of the subject of the locate without the permission of the subject.* This is true in general in reference to locates, but you are most at jeopardy and therefore need most to remember this guideline with the "friend" or "relative" search. Ask your client if he or she would be willing to give the subject of the search his or her

information. Often times, friends or relatives who have been out of touch will want to re-establish contact on their own grounds, in their own time. If you have a client who is sincerely interested in finding someone for legitimate reasons, he or she should not object to this type of exchange of information. As at least one private detective learned in the past, you can be found *instrumental* to the death of a person if your efforts were responsible for bringing the killer and victim together.

Witness Locates. A type of locate you'll want to make sure all your attorney clients know that you can perform. Along with Service of Process, domestic surveillance, and interviews/statements, witness locates are one of the primary services provided to attorneys by private detectives. For the most part, there will only be two types. Easy, because the client has substantial information about the witnesses already but has not contacted him or her as of yet. Difficult, because the attorney only knows the location where the incident took place and the date and time. If the situation is a difficult one, how difficult will depend on the neighborhood and your ability to talk to people. The nature of the incident can sometimes be a factor also, The more serious or heinous the incident, the stronger people will feel about it, and the more likely they will allow emotion to filter or alter what they saw. And, of course, in the age of ever-increasing apathy and conspicuous consumption, there will be those witnesses who "don't want to get involved."

Related to other types of investigations. As was stated earlier, most types of investigations will cultivate skills that can be used in other types of investigations. A certain percentage of times, related to anything ranging from service of process to surveillance, you may first need to locate a subject prior to being able to perform the work requested. **Do not** be shy in billing your client for the time it takes the locate to be accomplished. You should obtain his permission prior to starting and be reasonable as to billing for your time, but as long as you're being fair and your client believes you can get the job done, they will most often allow you to go ahead.

Missing children. Another form of personally rewarding locate investigations, these too will often require excellent communication skills more than anything else, primarily because the subject of the search does not have the same type of history an adult does. In the case of abductions, a good percentage of the abductions that occur are committed by a parent. With the increase in divorces that has permeated our society, there has been a corresponding increase in the number of parents dissatisfied with custody settlements. So, they sometimes opt to take matters into their own hands. The idea that a mother, father, or even grandparent or other relative would kidnap their own blood is far from unusual. These will require some level of coordination and cooperation with law enforcement. And, for the sake of the missing child and yourself, don't try to be the headline-grabbing hero. Let the police get the press. A well-known private detective once located the father who had taken his own child in violation of custody agreements and waited for the opportunity to grab the child. Of course, he was clever enough to ensure that no one could prove he did. His client's self-interest allowed her to give him the permission to act as he did. So, he never faced a kidnapping charge. But, the child whom he talked into coming with him for a drive across a few states now has not only emotional scars from the trauma of a divorce but also whatever trauma he might have experienced after he realized the nice man wasn't taking him back to daddy. No matter what anyone might say in defense of the actions of the detective, upon location of the father, law enforcement should have been notified and allowed to intervene. In the case of this type of abduction, they have the authority to arrest the father and return the child to the other parent. They also have more experience and a better support system to ensure everything is handled with as little disturbance to the child as possible. In certain circumstances, where the appropriate paperwork is produced, the other parent can authorize the private detective to transport the child back after the abducting parent has been arrested. Probably the most difficult aspect of this work, and runaways, is that you have to turn clients away who cannot afford to pay you. Pro bono and charity work has its place, after you've established yourself financially and to a limited degree. If you're a billionaire playboy with time on your hands, then do all you can. If you're a working stiff like most of us, do what you can that doesn't detract from your ability to live at least comfortably.

Runaways. Like missing children, there should be police reports filed, and you should talk to local law enforcement *prior* to accepting the investigation. The parents will all seem upset, depressed, distraught, and perhaps a little angry. Some of those parents, however, may have previous allegations of child abuse or neglect filed against them. Some of those allegations and/or charges may be unsupported or exaggerated. Some people believe that any form or corporal punishment is abuse. Another general rule to keep in mind is *don't allow your personal feelings or opinions to influence a business decision.* In as much as statistically very few private detectives are successfully civilly sued, protect your assets whenever possible. Local law enforcement, specifically the juvenile officers, should be able to provide you with a degree of insight into the family. In these cases, you will probably be talking to a variety of people—from friends to teachers to "the bad influences." Determine your approach, your manner of interviewing by the information you know about the runaway you're trying to find, and the background of the person you're going to talk to. The twenty-three year old, gang-affiliated, drug-trafficking-convicted male who is the romantic interest of the sixteen year old runaway requires a much different approach than the best friend's mother. Chances are you want to inform the adult romantic interest of all the possible criminal-charge implications in a firm but polite manner.

"Dead-beat" Parents. Not the most lucrative type of locate work at this time, this is a growing area for the private detective. The better percentage of these people are actually not capable of making the payments, as opposed to not willing to make the payments. There are those cases of clever people who have money and other assets well-hidden, though. With all the other things that law enforcement and the Office of the State's Attorney has to do, the location of these "dead-beats" and their subsequent arrest or payment of amounts outstanding is not the easiest thing. Locates are usually time-consuming, if not necessarily complex. One advantage we have over law enforcement and related fields is time. To say we're smarter, more capable, or better in any way than law enforcement or related agencies is nothing short of ludicrous. We do use different sources, and we do learn alternative methods of obtaining information, but they also do not have the luxury of dedicated time. And, in the case of those "dead-beat" parents who *do* have something to hide, more often than not they will have attempted to take as many careful measures as possible to ensure they, or least their assets, cannot be found. Unfortunately, it is most

often true that the more they have to hide, the easier it is for them to make it look as if they have nothing. Attorneys, accountants, doctors, or anyone who earns the same type of salary as these professionals will either know themselves how to hide assets or will know someone they can pay to do it. Take this for instances from our files: up to two years prior to his divorce, an attorney showed records that he was earning nearly fifty-thousand a year for seven years, and his firm was grossing nearly five hundred thousand. After that time, which just happened to be around the same time his father's will was altered to exclude the inheritance from being used for alimony, maintenance, or any other form of support, and approximately the same time the attorney obtained a new secretary, his reported income dropped such that, by the time the divorce was initiated, his paperwork showed him making twenty-thousand a year, with no other assets or holdings, and his company was now only seven-hundred and fifty dollars in the black. Can drastic events cause something like this to actually happen? Yes, you can never be sure you'll be or remain successful. In this case, however, it was careful planning, not bad luck, that put the attorney and his firm in such apparent dire straits.

Two factors that will greatly affect your level of success with most true locate investigations will be **how much information your client can provide, and whether or not the subject of the locate is actually trying to hide.** What we refer to as a true locate is an investigation to locate an individual who is currently trying to hide for one reason or another or an investigation in which substantial, current information is not readily available.

With the onset of the computerized information age, there are many legitimate companies who can provide locate-type services at a greatly reduced rate. The reason, primarily, is that these companies function merely as data-base companies, and as long as you have such identifiers as the subject's social security number, date of birth, last known address, driver's license number, they do a good job. However, when the subject has actually taken active steps to prevent people finding him, or, as in the case of an adoption search, when information of an exact, identifier-type number is not readily available, no computer will find your subject. When these subjects are being sought in relation to monies owed or similar matters, they are often referred to as a skip-trace. Skip-trace is terminology that arose out of collections actions. Persons who continually moved or took other measures so that they could continue to get credit were deemed "skips".

With the true locate, which usually can't be performed successfully simply by accessing a database, there are two *sources* of information.

- ***Offices, Organizations, Associations.*** The Freedom of Information Act of 1974, which is continually reinterpreted, requiring you to keep up with the changes, made certain information accessible to the general public. Commonly referred to as *public access information*, this is information that is obtained through any branch of local, state or federal government. There are other places that offer or can provide information. This writing does not attempt to list them all. Other writers have already compiled lists of places to write/go for information, and they have put them in the format of a reference book. These sources, such as the Clerk of the Circuit Court's Office, should be viewed as building blocks that will assist or direct your investigation. It is not very often that they will actually be the final step to locating a person. More often than not, they will help to establish some identifying numbers on your subject, reveal possible alternative addresses, and, most importantly, provide you with the names (and, hopefully addresses and phone numbers) of persons who would have some interest in knowing where your subject is hanging his or her hat.
- ***People.*** With true locates, locates that are not simply a matter of using a postal forwarding to obtain a new address, you will have to talk to a few people in order to end your search. Whether it is a father, sister, friend, ex-employer, ex-neighbor, or ex-landlord, a successful interview will most often determine your overall success. The nature of the locate investigation, and, at times, the nature of the relation to the subject of the locate investigations, will determine whether you interview under *pretext* or in a straightforward manner. Either way, the ability to effectively communicate with a variety of people is a necessary skill to be a successful locate investigator.

Some of the sources of public access and other information before leaving the office.

- *411/Telephone or internet.* Never overlook the obvious; your client may have. And, while this will mean you'll make less money if it's that simple, you now have a client who is even more grateful. Also, you will always want to *verify the information you've been given*—clients have been known to confuse information by transposing numbers or similar mistakes. Saving an hour and a half of driving., especially in Chicago where the driving seasons are only winter and road construction, is worth the time spent. (Nationwide phone directories are now available on CD-ROM).

- *Reverse directory.* If the phone number is non-published, this service will not be of any assistance. But, there are no guarantees to any type of source, so you take your shots with each. Again, a simple phone call or check on the internet *may* save a trip. 796-9600 is the number within the Chicago Metro area for the reverse directory of the telephone company that provides name and address information for a given phone number. Some areas will not have this type of service available. In most instances, however, you should be able to purchase reverse directory books for Dontech/Donnelly.
- *Criss-cross index.* The criss-cross index service is available through the reference section of most public libraries. Normally, the better the library, the more sources the personnel there will be able to use (for most of the North and Northwest suburbs of Chicago, the Arlington Heights library is the best source; the Harold Washington library is the best for the city of Chicago proper). You simply call the library, ask for the reference section, and tell the person from the reference section that you wish to have criss-cross check performed. They will know what you want. Give them the address that you have, and they will tell you the name and phone number listed with that address, if the information is available. A multi-unit building should not present a problem because information for each unit will be listing as for a separate address.

These three steps should be the first taken on any locate, to a certain degree to attempt to locate, but more so to verify information given to you by the client. It is not often that these steps will locate your subject, but quite often they will save you time and money you may have spent based on outdated information or a simple transposed numbers. Clients do make mistakes. And, sometimes, such as with attorney-clients, the information that you are getting has already passed through at least two other channels, allowing for further errors in communication.

Some of the sources of public access and other information at the courthouse.

- *The Clerk of the Circuit Court.* (For those operating in the Chicago Metro area, you should remember that Cook County is an anomaly because of its size in relation to population; as of this writing, the authors have found no other county in the State of Illinois that requires the investigator to travel to more than one location to obtain various files.) The Clerk of the Circuit Court's Office can provide various information and should be located in the county courthouse. There may be some variations as to how each office is set up and the procedures to obtain certain information, but, for the most part, the information that you are allowed to access should be the same.

    a.) *Criminal Records.* Look through all the paperwork in the criminal file (arrest report, follow-up investigative report, court docket, bond sheet, etc.). Currently, those online services that provide criminal history information for background investigations cannot provide a complete file without taking extra time and charging extra money. If a person were bailed out by someone else, that other person will have motivation to know where the subject is. A court docket may reveal an upcoming court date. As with all records, search thoroughly; the information you may need for this locate will not necessarily be in the same place as the last locate.

    b.) *Civil Records.* You will again be looking for information about your subject, about those people who may have reason to know where your subject is, and about future court dates. With civil searches you will be able to search for your subject either as plaintiff or defendant.

    c.) *Traffic offenses.* Often overlooked, these may reveal the most current address and vehicle information about your subject. There may be occasions when the address on the ticket is one that you already know and have been to, only to be told the subject no longer lives there or that the subject is not known to the residents. But, you may also see that the vehicle the subject was driving is one that you noticed parked in the driveway.

Generally speaking, it is more likely that the average person has received a traffic ticket as opposed to being arrested for criminal offenses.

- *The County Clerk's Office* is a separate and distinct office from the Clerk of the Circuit Court. The Clerk of the Circuit Court is an office responsible for maintaining records of activities in that Circuit and so is not necessarily limited to one county and is not responsible for the same types of records as the County clerk:

    a) *Marriage records.* This may be one of the easiest ways for a woman to change her name. This is not to say that being married is easy, but the paperwork aspects are brief. Depending upon the size of the county, you may actually have to search the files by hand. The nature of the investigation will determine whether or not you will want to pay exorbitant fees for a copy/certified copy. In most instances, write up notes of any worthwhile information.

    b) *Divorce records.* These records can prove substantially informative, particularly in the instance of contested divorces. The more people argue, normally, the more of their "laundry" is made public via the divorce proceedings. Information in relation to assets (including vehicles, real estate, business owned, stocks, etc.) will often be listed so that the court can determine what is to be divided/distributed and how. Information in relation to children will be included within these records normally. Particularly in those instances where child support and "maintenance" are considerations, at least one party will be required to produce records to substantiate their entire financial status.

- *The Recorder of Deeds.* Quite often used in relation to the location of assets, this office can prove useful in the location of persons also. For every action that occurs in relation to a parcel of property, there should be a record within the offices of the Recorder of Deeds. From the sale of a parcel to an inspection by the Health Department, there should be a record. Related to this office in a way, the **Tax Assessor's** office is another office to check in relation to property and ownership. We have found a number of occasions where the person/entity listed as the owner with the county was not the same person paying the taxes. More often than not, people do not pay the taxes for property that they hold no interest in.

Stepping away from the county offices, there are numerous other places where the investigator can obtain information. For most of these offices, and the county offices as well, there will be a computer terminal—with instructions for those of us who may be a step of two behind the times—for use. You will enter the name, the computer will search for matching files, and you will have to ask the clerk for those files. Once again, a good investigator should not be caught without a pen and paper.

- *City Hall.* Even if your personal tendency is to fight city hall, professionally you will find that their offices can be quite helpful. From business licenses to all kind of permits, a lot of information may be found at city hall. Like most of the other places we will discuss, it can't be found over the phone. If an individual had his name changed legally, those records would be located either in city hall or the county building. With city hall, you may have to use a Freedom of Information Request, but even then, you will obtain whatever information is on file. And, most cities have a form you can fill out as opposed to having to draft a request.
- *Secretary of State.* Of course, there may be variations from state to state, but, you can check the books listed in the *Recommended Reading* chapter to determine if your state varies greatly from Illinois. The Secretary of State's Department of Corporations can be accessed via telephone and will tell you information in relation to a corporation such as its listed officers (at least President, Secretary, and Registered Agent), address(es) and current standing. There is also a taxation division that can inform you as to whether or not the taxes have been paid. The Secretary of State's Office is more helpful in those instances when you are working for an attorney because as the agent of an attorney you can obtain driver's license abstracts and vehicle registration and title information. Both of these can be very helpful when you have little information about the subject of your search.
- *(Dirksen) Federal Building.* Federal buildings will not be located in every city or county for that matter. In Illinois, there are three—Chicago, Peoria, and Springfield. The Dirksen is in the

Loop. Federal court records, as well as bankruptcy records, are available through these offices. The Fed also offers one of the few true on-line systems, called P.A.C.E.R. For the cost of any normal modem-related service, you can search the records from your office to see if your subject has ever filed bankruptcy, or was involved with Federal litigation.

- *State of Illinois Building/Thompson Center.* Obviously, the name will change from state to state. But, located in this building, within the offices of the Illinois Industrial Commission, are records in relation to workers' compensation claims. Like a criminal, civil, or divorce file, these records will have a significant amount of information in relation to the person at the time the claim was filed. And, there may be an indication that the company is still paying the person for the injury sustained. If so, they will most likely have this address.

- *The State of Illinois Department of Financial and Professional Regulation.* Almost every state will have a similar office, perhaps with a different name. This is the place you can call or write to find out if the private detective you hired is legitimate. The Department can tell you over the phone if a person is licensed and whether or not the license has ever been disciplined in any way. Details of any action taken against the license cannot be given over the phone, but you can find those out through a formal written request. The Department is not only responsible for private detectives but also private security contractors, private alarm contractors, locksmiths, real estate agents, certain medical personnel (certified nursing associates, etc.), and other licensed or certified professions within the state. Generally speaking, the stricter the state guidelines are for a profession, the greater likelihood that information will be accessible.

These are not the only places/offices available where one can obtain information. I have included a recommended reading chapter that includes the names of some of those books. The information that you may be able to obtain from these various offices will most often act as building blocks, bringing you closer to your subject and developing a profile. For the most part, especially when your subject is trying to hide or in the instance of something like an adoption search where there is minimal information to start with, you will have to rely on these files revealing someone who can tell you where this person is. For that reason, your communication skills are of particular importance with locate investigations. In the instance wherein the client has a substantial amount of accurate information about the subject, and the subject is not actively trying to hide, it may be as simple as a postal forwarding request or a search through the nationwide phone directory disc. Those searches will be significantly less complicated, less costly, and, therefore are hardly a true test of your skills as a locate investigator.

The interview. Although there will be cases other than locates that require interviews, interview techniques are an important aspect of the locate investigation. The nature of the locate and the relationship of the person to be interviewed to the "subject" of the locate investigation should be what determines the style of interview used. **All** interviews, no matter the type of investigation, should have the same underlying principles as regards being prepared, remembering psychological, sociological, emotional and motivational factors, and **taking notes.**

Definition of the interview (*not necessarily according to Webster*). A conversation with an individual whom you have reason to believe is aware of information that is pertinent to your investigation. For locates in particular, the interview should have a conversational aspect. That is to say, while you should have prepared questions, and you want to maintain a degree of control, the conversation needs to be allowed to take the direction that is most likely to produce worthwhile information. It **should not,** with rare exceptions, take on the rigorous, rigid structure of an interrogation. Some general guidelines and important factors to be remembered that will help you be a more successful interviewer:

1) Attempt to establish a relaxed atmosphere. Whether done so by location, personal presentation, or even the use of pretext where appropriate, it *is* important that a person feels relaxed. Remember, they may be doing you a favor, so it is important that they feel comfortable in doing so.
2) Human Behavior/Psychology. Listed below are some of the more obvious aspects of psychological considerations; one of the reasons you can always learn more and never become an expert in this field is that (yes, even before there were psychologists or psychiatrists) it has been proven there is no definite formula to human behavior. And, like barbers, salesmen, family doctors or other "people persons,"

there is always a new insight to getting a job done quicker and/or easier. A last note to remember is that, when you are watching what people do/how they behave for indicators or insights, remember people will be processing information about you both consciously and sub-consciously, based upon how to present yourself. This will affect their reactions to you and your inquiries.

> A.) *Distance.* All people have reactions to the relative closeness of another person. Initially, you will want to maintain a certain distance (at least four or five feet from the subject). Then, through observation of the individual, and remembering the nature of the investigation, determine whether you should move closer, maintain your distance, or even step backward a few more feet.
>
> B.) *Eye movement.* "The eyes are the windows to the soul" is actually taken from Bram Stoker's Dracula. Eye movement and eye contact are good reflectors of an emotional reaction or deception. As with all factors of this nature, remember you have to establish the individual pattern and use the average (35%-60% of a normal conversation) only as a general guideline.
>
> C.) *Verbal.* Tone, pitch, volume, rate, and word choice are all factors of speech that, when changing, often reflect an emotional reaction and/or the attempt to be deceptive. For instance, when the person who has been using collegiate vocabulary suddenly slips into a monosyllabic, slang vocabulary, there is the distinct probability that the last question asked "struck a nerve." Here again, and particularly here, remember that the subjects will be watching and listening too. If there is, and there usually will be, a certain way that you could present yourself to obtain results, then give that subject the angry, sad or indifferent person they need to see in order to give any information.
>
> D.) *Personalization.* Whether through preparation by studying the person's available background information or by on-site observation of personal effects at the location, attempt to appropriately interject personal comments. If you're walking up the driveway and you see a fishing pole in the back seat of the car, ask them where they've been fishing, what they've been catching. Do you really care? No. Might you be making the

person more relaxed? Yes. Does this make you look more like their kind of people? Yes. If the person knocking at your door and asking you questions is from your high school, college, or home town; if he's been working on his house or garden and could use some information; if he talks like the people whom you consider to be "regular people," are you more likely to talk with him?

E.) *The need to feel important.* Everyone, no matter what someone might tell you, likes to feel important. So, you might want to make the person you're speaking to be **the person** who can help you resolve this investigation. Or, combining personalization factors with this idea, you could ask his or her advice on something. Whenever someone is perceived as an advisor, teacher, or expert, he or she almost automatically feels important and is more inclined to discourse at length. Yes, this might cause that person to go off the subject of your interest for a moment, but you should be able to guide him or her back to it without abruptly stopping the rambling. Rambling is something you have to learn to put up with, as long as you're getting some useful information along the way that is.

There will be those people who are being deceptive, and hopefully through your observations you will realize this at the time. Depending upon the circumstances of the investigation, and particularly their relation to the subject you are hoping to find, you will either need to make those people feel more comfortable and less threatened or more nervous. Some of the people you might speak with, for instance, will want to give you information but feel they can't for reasons of personal safety. If you believe that this is true, assure them that a good private detective never reveals sources. And, a *good private detective* **does not** *reveal sources.*

Remember, proper preparation prevents poor performance. Whenever possible, have questions prepared and always include a series of initial "set" questions. These are questions that most people would answer truthfully (name, occupation, etc.) and are used so that you can establish what the normal behavioral patterns are for that person. Find out as much information as you can about the individual prior to the interview—as much as with other investigations, knowledge is power. Sometimes, your knowledge of the person in and of itself will make the person feel that they should talk to you. And, it can also make the person aware of the fact that they should not attempt to be deceptive, particularly when you can point out something you know to be true right after they've attempted to deceive you.

Remember, people are generally creatures of habit.

Remember, even if you don't have the time or resources to research an individual, most people do have some aspects of their personality that are related to general "categories" or "types." Being careful not to accept these as facts or always, *in general it is true that,* for instance, the average female is more likely to exhibit emotion than the average male who may not want people to know he's sensitive. The average college student will know less about certain realities of the world than the average blue collar worker of the same age. *Again, these are generalizations: not absolutes, not always true, just based on averages.*

Finally, remember that these are general guidelines, and the key to successful interviewing is your own ability to adapt to the circumstances. If there was a simple set of ground rules that would guarantee successful interviewing, there would not be the myriad of "experts" espousing their methodology that exists in our industry and others.

Coordination and cooperation with law enforcement. Certain types of locates that the private detective is retained to perform will eventually require the involvement of law enforcement personnel. These are

- Runaways,
- Missing children, and
- Dead-beat parents.

Although these types of locates will originate from an individual/personal client, each will necessarily require that you coordinate with police prior to the initiation of the inestigation and upon successful location of the "subject."

1) Prior to the initiation of the investigation—establishing contact at the outset serves more than one purpose.

   (a) To establish the validity of your clients request.
   (b) To obtain police report or warrant information that will be necessary when contacting law enforcement upon completion.
   (c) To obtain any information that law enforcement might have to assist in your investigation.

2) Upon successfully locating your "suspect" in these types of locates, you will need to contact law enforcement so that they can dispatch someone to apprehend your suspect, or, in the case of a runaway or a missing child who was abducted by a parent, take the runaway or child into their custody to ensure his or her safety and return. Law enforcement has been far better trained in these areas and will have support service personnel (social workers, juvenile detectives, etc) who can help the run-away or missing child in more ways than you can).

The Proverbial Brick Wall. There are two issues to be brought forth in terms of the problem of running into the proverbial "brick wall," which will happen quite often. The first is, "What do I know about the suspect I am trying to locate?" and the second is, "What will my client spend to have this person found?"

1.) What do I know about the suspect?

  (a) No matter what else might be true about locate investigations, one truth is that you cannot count on any two being the same. That is, where you might find the information that leads you to a person who can lead you to your suspect is never certain.

   i) Suspect's work—would have reason to be licensed or obtain permits. Is his work specialized, seasonal, or likely to be done only in certain areas?
   ii) Suspect's education—friends/alumni club
   iii) Suspect's family
   iv) Suspect's hobbies, free-time activities

2.) Depending upon what you know, you may have to sit surveillance at a local tavern or make a lot of phone calls. But, if you break everything down to each aspect of the person's life and examine the possible sources, there is a way to get around almost all brick walls. And, you will want to get around or over them, not try to go through them.

3.) Persistence is necessary. Curiosity, the desire to know for your own sake, is necessary. Much like circumstances often encountered with a difficult surveillance, a resolution may be reached only after some careful, creative thinking.

(a) What is my client willing to pay?

4.) Clients do need to be treated fairly, and service is a substantial aspect of that. Communication needs to be constant, direct, and honest. The best advice I ever received from someone I worked for was to remember that this is a business, not Same Spade or Jim Rockford. Inform your client of what your best estimate of the costs to continue will be and then allow the client to make his or her best judgment as to whether or not to proceed. This is the ethical, professional manner of proceeding. There may be those times when you perform pro bono work, but, to the best of my knowledge, there are no non-profit detective agencies.

Another point with these types of investigations: a percentage of clients who desire locate oriented investigations (adoptions, missing friends, runaways) will be people who will desire to talk to you at great length, people who want an ear to bend and a counselor of sorts. Give them that ear, and be aware of reputable counselors in the area. Recommending a good counselor to people in an emotionally charged circumstance should be your last service provided for this type of client. It is a good way to relieve yourself of the responsibility.

A final business word: locates are challenging, can be personally rewarding, and should be fun. But, remember that a detective agency is a business like any other business. Your desire to help people or be the person who found someone no one else could has to be balanced by the necessity of paying bills. Having your own license will allow you discretion will allow you to drop a certain percentage of the hours you worked on an investigation if you want to make the bill one that doesn't cripple your client.

CASE FILES: When Looking for Lost Loved Ones, Sometimes It Pays to Advertise

The smell of bacon frying, coffee brewing and fresh baking was always something I liked. I was sitting in the small restaurant, sipping my third cup of coffee, lighting my second cigarette and talking to Lou Ann, who was more than happy to tell me about most anything that had happened in Sikeston in the last ten years or so.

There is a certain laid-back, relaxed style and atmosphere about people in the Southern States. When I had been back in the Chicago metro area, doing most of the advance work for this adoption investigation, there was a part of me that secretly hoped we would not be successful in locating our client's brother through our efforts over phone and fax. Despite being raised and trained in the investigation industry in the big city and surrounding crowded suburbs, I had always like working in the South. The people were always more open, more willing to talk, and whether they knew you or not, you were always greeted with a "Good mornin'. How are 'ya?"

Sikeston was that same way, and in the last twenty five hours I had managed to talk to Lou Ann and two other people who were more than happy to talk to a "big city detective." Of course, I had to explain that Magnum was a far cry from reality, and adding a light Southern drawl to my voice probably helped. It's a strange thing, though, because before I went to Ft. McClellan, Alabama for my Military Police Training or served my time in El Paso, Texas, I had already had people asking me where my Southern drawl came from. And, for the most part, except perhaps when you were talking to a family member of a fugitive in a bail enforcement related investigation, the drawl or more elaborate pretexting wasn't really necessary. Southern folks just take it natural to help where they can.

Lou Ann herself wasn't actually able to provide much information about the family I was searching for. She didn't know the Hadens, nor had she heard talk of them. She was fairly young, though, and the adoptions had occurred over 30 years ago. Lou Ann did tell me to check over to the grade school, which I had already planned to do, that the Dixons had been one of the first families to settle into Sikeston, and that I ought to go over to have a talk with old Samuel. As Lou Ann put it, "He knows about everything that's happened and everyone that's been down to Sikeston in the last sixty years."

I finished three more cups of coffee, two eggs, grits and sausage while talking to Lou and two men who came in about Sikeston, politics and the country in general. Their conversation was not couched in hesitated political correctness or limited by carefully guarded personal opinions. From there I proceeded to the grade school where I was allowed to look at yearbooks that would have reflected the children attending at the time our client was adopted. He had been told his birth name by his adoptive mother, but his brother had been adopted into another family. The yearbooks revealed three possible children bearing a resemblance. A quick check of the phonebook revealed that only one of the families still lived in Sikeston. Having this possibly-related knowledge in hand, I decided to talk to Samuel over some iced tea. After all, it was getting to be quite a scorcher.

Samuel was more than happy to talk to me. Unfortunately, while he did know the family that was still in town, he also knew that they had had only one child, and the mother had died in childbirth. Nonetheless, I talked with Samuel a while longer after learning this, enjoying the descriptive, story-telling quality of his conversation.

From Samuel's house, I went back to the Super Eight motel and called the office. I informed my partner Dave of what I had been able to determine so far, and he and I both agreed that a little bit of the power of advertising might work. While I had been over to the diner, I had asked Lou Ann and a couple of other people what was the best paper in town, and they indicated that the *Standard Democrat* was the most read. I called their offices and found out that today was their "circulation day," the day when everyone gets a paper in an effort to get everyone to subscribe, and that if I could get the classified ad over in the next hour and a half they could get it into the day's paper.

After I had left the small offices of the *Standard Democrat*, having submitted the advertisement for anyone who had any information about our client's family, I proceeded to go to the six locations of families with the same family birth name of our client, on the possibility that talking to them in person might produce a different result. I drove on highways and dirt roads, from places that looked like the stereotypical country, cozy home to others that looked like a scene from "Deliverance." Having no success, I proceeded to the county seat to check marriage, divorce, death and other records to see if I could discover any information.

By the time I got back to my motel room, a little less confident that this case would be closed within 72 hours, there were five messages. Three of them were from the office, one was from a woman who claimed to know all about our client's family, and the other from a man who said he knew where our client's mother was. I called the office first, confirming with my partner that there had been a strong response to the ad that had given the office number. Dave had told the two people who called of the motel and room I was in.

I first called the woman who stated she knew all about the family. When I first spoke to her, there was a noticeable degree of hesitation in her voice. I asked her a series of questions without revealing any information about our client, and she wanted to ask me a series of questions. I asked her if I could answer her questions in person; her responses indicated to me that she was quite well aware of our client's family history. She explained that she ran the diner in the little town just west of Sikeston, that she was just getting ready to close up, but if I wanted to come right over, she'd put on a pot of coffee. I told her I never turned down a good cup of coffee.

It was seven-thirty when I got over to the diner. By nine o'clock, she had determined that I was sincere by seeing my identification, and I had determined that she was our client's half sister whom he didn't even know existed. She had been willing to have her husband bring over her birth certificate showing her birth name, as well as a set of photographs of our client, his brothers whom he knew as they were adopted into the same family, as well as his sister, and another brother whom neither he nor his brothers were sure was an accurate aspect of their memory.

We were both anxious and happy. I called our client at home from the diner and talked to him for a while, giving him the information slowly, and then turned the phone over to Marybeth. They talked for almost an hour. The next day, I got to meet our client's sister, who had also always wondered about her siblings and considered such a search, but was never sure if maybe everyone was better left in the dark.

Two weeks after my trip down to Sikeston, there was a very emotional family reunion in Sikeston. Since that time, Penny and Jimmy have visited Chicago a number of times. There were, as there sometimes tends to be, some painful discoveries about their parents, but in this case there was an overriding sense of celebration.

Generally speaking, no two locate investigations will be the same, at least in the sense that you can hardly predict that source, that person, or that effort will close the case. In this particular instance, and in other cases of a similar nature, especially in small towns where families tend to put down roots and generations of the same family will remain, the power of advertising can be tremendous in resolving a locate investigation.

CHAPTER FIVE

Surveillance, A True Test of Patience and Persistence

Surveillance is the continuous observation of persons, places and things so as to obtain information regarding the activities and identities of individuals. This is the definition as it applies to the actual surveillance investigation. That is, when performing a surveillance, to obtain that information is the primary objective. As with other types of investigations, surveillance is also an investigative skill used to successfully complete other investigations where the detective was not hired specifically or primarily to perform surveillance. A locate, service of process or even a bail enforcement investigation, for instance, might require the detective to put in a couple of hours in order to effect the serve or positively identify the subject's location. In the same way, although you were hired to perform a surveillance in relation to a fraudulent workers' compensation claim, your client might not have current address information, requiring you to perform a locate in order to conduct your surveillance. There is a substantial amount of money to be made in this industry by specializing, especially in surveillance. However, you should remember, it is quite often true that **specializing has the effect of putting limits on yourself, thereby restricting your own ability to grow.**

Knowledge is power. Investigators on surveillance assignments *must* have complete knowledge of overall objectives and full familiarity with descriptive data relating to all places, persons, and vehicles believed to be related to the investigation. Investigators conducting these types of assignments should have knowledge of the traffic conditions around an area, of road constructions, of the possible routes to and from known destinations of a subject, etc. These investigators will encounter continuously changing problems, which makes the investigator's ability to accurately recall essential details much more important. This consideration depends to a great degree upon the investigator's powers of observation. All of that will be reflected in the final products—video, photographs and reports. To a certain degree in the "private sector," whether or not you have repeat business will be based on your reports. And, the camcorder, like any other tool, is just a tool. The skill is in the mind of the investigator who uses the knowledge given to effectively react to the circumstances that occur as the surveillance is being conducted.

Never assume that the clients have provided you all the information they have. Even if you are an entry level investigator being given an assignment by a supervisor, ask as many questions as you can think of that might pertain to getting the assignment accomplished. If your boss knows you're thinking, that's a good thing.

Despite what anyone might tell you, *you will lose visual contact with a subject on occasion*—**this is not the end of the investigation.** If you know some of the places the subject might be going to (where they work out, where they usually get a coffee, or a drink, or go fishing/bowling, etc.) and have an idea that they're headed in that general direction, you can proceed and hope to re-establish contact. The more you know about your subject, the greater likelihood you have of a successful surveillance investigation

Self Confidence. Successful surveillance is largely dependent upon the investigator's self confidence. The investigator must be able to assume the appearance *and* actions, under any and all circumstances, of any ordinary citizen confronted with the problems created by the existing environment. The investigator must make decisions that do not give the appearance of either hesitation or the unusual. While it is important to remember that there are ways to change your outward, physical appearance, and they are often recommended, your actions and reactions to normal and unusual circumstances or situations have to reinforce, rather than contradict, the less-than-noteworthy image you are attempting to project. Second-guessing yourself will often lead only to your taking unusual actions to alter the current action/direction you have taken. Re-evaluating upon completion of the assignment is always a good idea; there is always room for improvement.

However, you should be confident that under the given circumstances your judgment will ensure success.

Equipment Check. Proper preparation prevents poor performance—just one of the infamous expressions prevalent in the military, law enforcement and the private sector. Surveillance *equipment* goes beyond a camera and/or camcorder. You should have a mini tape recorder to allow you to concentrate on driving and following the subject as opposed to having to worry about taking notes. A voice activated recorder is preferable, especially where you want to just keep it on the passenger seat to talk to. You will have to decide if talking to yourself or holding the mini-recorder to your mouth will appear unusual. While driving the Kennedy and other highways, toll ways, and roads around the Chicago Metro area, it is not at all unusual to see someone talking to a mini-recorder, but at the same time, it does cause people to momentarily look at you. And, if they should have other reasons to take notice of you or observe you a number of times over a lengthy period, they may "make" you. A map-book is always a good idea to have as a backup in case you encounter problems with your GPS device. Binoculars should be standard equipment. At least two changes of clothes should be brought with. This will allow for two things; you can alter the picture of the person in your subject's rear-view mirror (hats and glasses work particularly well as most people tend to focus on these types of features, and they alter the appearance of your facial structure), and you are capable of changing into clothing that will be more appropriate to the setting if your subject leaves from a conservative, business location and goes to a casual location. For men, a milk bottle will help if you are necessarily required to be stationary for long periods of time. You won't be able to leave the vehicle to use the facilities. Food and drink are a good idea because you can't be sure that you'll have the opportunity to get any during the course of the surveillance. You should always have spare film for your still camera and a battery charger or spare charged battery for your camcorder; you can never have too many pictures or too much film when out in the field. What is unnecessary will be determined after the assignment is completed.

The Surveillance Vehicle. What should be first and foremost in the mind of the investigator in regards to a vehicle to be used for surveillance is the same idea as their own appearance: *the vehicle should not draw the attention of the average person.* Vans, mini-vans, and "sport utility" vehicles are quite popular, so they do not stand out more than the average sedan or coupe (well, for now, but the record profits of oil companies is already having an effect on that). For what is expected to be a stationary surveillance, or primarily a stationary surveillance, a van is the better option because it does allow you to be more easily hidden in the rear area, as well as allowing for slight movement within the vehicle and more room for various equipment. If the anticipation is that the surveillance will be of the mobile (the traditional "tail") type, on the other hand, vans and similar vehicles are not always the best option. ***Personalized plates are not an option.*** For the surveillance investigator, and really for investigators in general, personalized plates are like flashing neon. There are other items the investigator, surveillance and in general, should stay away from as a general rule:

a) *Bumper stickers.* Again, these will only serve to more positively identify your vehicle in the mind of the general public. Obviously one sticker, such as a Bulls sticker for those living in the Chicago area, may not be seriously detrimental. One sticker that professionally may prove helpful is the popular "My child is an honor student at . . ." Now, if you lose the subject early in the morning and there were children in the car, you have a good chance of reestablishing contact.

b) *Antennae.* Having radio communication is always preferable when working a surveillance with a team, but most vehicles do not have more than a stereo antenna.

c) *License plate decorations.* Whether it's the neon glow or the chains around the plate, having people notice your vehicle in general is bad, drawing attention to your license plate is even worse.

d) *Excessive damage, rust, etc.* Admittedly, it is difficult to keep any car in "mint" condition no matter where you live. However, a small ding on the door is substantially different than the quarter panel of a red vehicle being covered with gray primer.

Foot surveillance. Although foot surveillance is not often the primary focus of an investigation, because it is also a consideration of most other surveillance investigations, I felt it appropriate to begin with foot surveillance when discussing the procedural aspects of performing these investigations. By this I mean that while other investigations will call for you to be primarily focused on vehicular or stationary surveillance, both of these are also likely to require that you include a certain amount of foot surveillance to complete the investigation.

In general, the procedural guidelines discussed with respect to foot surveillance will be similar to those you apply for other surveillance. The primary objective is to maintain the surveillance while eluding detection. So, while there will be those procedures that obviously do not directly translate from foot to vehicle, the principles involved are essentially the same.

1. One-man foot surveillance

    (a) Surveillance is extremely difficult for one man and *should be avoided if possible.*
    (b) The subject must be kept in sight at all times.
    (c) One-man surveillance will usually be very close and partially dependent on pedestrian traffic along with physical characteristics of the area.
    (d) Investigator should be on the same side of the street as the subject.
    (e) It is crucial for the investigator to be near enough to immediately observe the subject if he turns a corner, enters a building, etc.

2. Two-man surveillance

    (a) The use of two investigators allows greater security against detection and decreases the risk of losing the subject.
    (b) On streets dense with pedestrian and vehicular traffic, both investigators will usually remain on the same side of the street as the subject:

        (1) The first investigator tailing the subject fairly close.
        (2) The second investigator trailing the first investigator a good distance behind.

    (c) On less crowded streets, one investigator may walk on the opposite side of the road nearly parallel to the subject.
    (d) In order to avoid being noticed, investigators, should make occasional changes in their positions relative to the subject.

3. Three-man surveillance (ABC method)

   (a) The use of three investigators further reduces the risk of losing the subject and, under ordinary circumstances, permits even greater security against detection.
   (b) The three-man method allows a greater variation in the position of the investigators and also gives any one investigator the option to drop out if spotted.

   (1) Use of the ABC method under normal traffic conditions.

       (a) The "A" investigator stays a reasonable distance behind the subject.
       (b) The "B" investigator follows "A" and focuses on keeping "A" in sight.
       (c) The "C" investigator walks on the opposite side of the street just behind the subject.
       (d) The "B" investigator is also responsible for detecting any confederate of the subject to detect surveillance.

   (2) Use of the ABC method on the streets with little or no traffic.

       (a) Two investigators may be on opposite sides of the street, or
       (b) One investigator may be in front of the subject.

   (3) Use of the ABC method on very crowded streets.

       (a) All three investigators should generally be on the same side of the street.
       (b) The lead investigator will follow close to the subject to monitor his direction at intersections and entryways.

   (4) As in the two-man method, the investigators should frequently alter their positions relative to the subject.
   (5) Under normal traffic conditions, when the subject approaches a street intersection, the "C" investigator

should lead the subject and reach the intersection first, pausing at the corner or crossing the street, watching the subject and signaling to "A" and "B" the subject's actions after he passes from sight. If he signals that the subject has stopped, the "A" investigator should cross the intersection before proceeding in the direction the subject did when he turned the corner. If the subject pauses several moments, both "A" and "B" investigators may have to proceed to a point outside of subjects view. Investigator "C" could then signal "A" and "B" when subject continues moving. The subject turning a corner can be used as an opportunity for investigators to rotate positions regardless of whether or not the subject stops.

(6) Three to five investigators are often used with the ABC method. Six to eight investigators can also be used; however, more than that can cause the team to become unwieldy.

4. Progressive or "leap frog" method of surveillance.

   (a) Use of this method is uncommon because of the time involved and the poor chances of obtaining good results.
   (b) It involves the observation of the subject as he progresses along a certain route, with the investigator stationing himself at a fixed point until the subject disappears from view.
   (c) If the subject follows the same route each day, a destination can be determined without following the subject if the investigator positions himself each day at the location where he lost sight of the subject.
   (d) Disadvantages.

      (1) No guarantee that the subject will follow the same route each day.
      (2) No guarantee that the subject will go to the same destination each day.

5. Combined foot surveillance.

(a) This method involved surveillance by one, two or three investigators and additional surveillance simultaneously by one or two investigators in an automobile.
(b) Through this method, investigators will always be assured of transportation if the subject should board a bus, streetcar or taxicab.
(c) Several investigators can also be carried in the car, and the investigators on foot can be frequently changed to avoid compromise.
(d) Caution must be exercised in the operation of the automobile as a slow moving car may become conspicuous.

Foot surveillance problems

1. Subject enters building:

   (a) Typically, at least one investigator should follow the subject unless the building is of such a type that the entry would expose the investigator. (private home, small shop, etc.).
   (b) In the case of a large public building with many exits, all of the investigators should follow the subject into the building.
   (c) In buildings that the subject might be lost easily, it may be advisable to station one investigator at the door or in the lobby to spot the subject as they leave the building.

2. Subject enters an elevator:

   (a) If the subject is the one passenger and has reason to suspect surveillance, it may be best not to accompany him into the elevator but rather to watch the indicator for the floor stop and then proceed to that floor to try to pick up the subject's route.
   (b) In other cases one or two investigators may accompany the subject, wait for him to announce his floor and then ask for a higher or lower floor and use the stairs to get to the subject's floor and attempt to pick up his trail.
   (c) At all times one investigator should be left in the lobby since the subject may be using the elevator in an attempt to elude surveillance.

3. Subject enters restaurant:

    (a) At least one investigator should enter behind the subject, order approximately the same amount of food and be alert to note any contacts made by the subject.
    (b) If possible, the investigator should pay his check before the subject does so that he can be ready to leave with him.
    (c) In some cases, it may be desirable for the investigator to leave shortly before the subject and wait for him outside.

4. Subject boards a streetcar, bus or subway:

    (a) At least one investigator should board the same car or bus and sit behind or at least on the same side as the subject.
    (b) If an investigator should miss the streetcar or bus or should fear that by boarding it he might make the subject suspicious, he may hire a taxi to follow the car for the full distance or follow by taxi for a few blocks, overtake and then board the car.
    (c) The ideal practice is for one investigator to board the car or bus and for the others to follow in a surveillance automobile.

5. Subject takes a taxicab:

    (a) If trailing by another taxi or by surveillance automobile is impossible or impractical, the investigator should make a note of the time, the place, the name of the cab company and the license number or cab number.
    (b) The subject's destination can be determined later by checking with the driver or the company office.

6. Subject enters a telephone booth/goes to phone area:

    (a) One investigator should attempt to overhear the conversation by pretending to make a call from an adjacent phone or by pretending to look up a number in the directory.

7. Subject takes a train, boat, plane or long distance bus:

(a) Whether an investigator will follow his subject on any trip usually depends upon the indicated length of the trip and the instructions he has received from his superior.

(b) The subject's destination may be learned by listening while he is buying his ticket, by questioning the ticket agent or by contacting the conductor of the train.

8. Subject enters a theater, race track or amusement park:

   (a) All investigators should normally follow the subject.
   (b) The regular admission charges should be paid.
   (c) Investigators must follow the subject closely in order not to lose him in the crowd.
   (d) In darkened theaters, the subject must be watched closely and, if possible, one investigator should sit directly behind the subject to avoid losing him. The exits should also be covered to avoid losing him.

9. Subject meets a contact:

   (a) A complete detailed description of the contact should be noted, together with time and place of the meeting.
   (b) If possible, the contact should be photographed.
   (c) If practical, attempts should be made to overhear the conversation.
   (d) The subject's attitude toward the contact should be noted.

10. Subject registers at a motel:

    (a) The subject's room number may be obtained from the manager, house detective or room clerk.
    (b) If the hotel management is cooperative it may be possible to procure a room near the subject's that can be used as a base for technical surveillance.

11. Investigators lose subject:

    (a) The investigator in charge should be immediately notified.

(b) Known hangouts or addresses frequented by the subject should be placed under observation immediately in an effort to find him.
(c) It is generally advisable to station an investigator in the area where the subject was last seen, as he may reappear there after a short time.
(d) Phone calls may be made to home or places frequented by the subject under a pretext and will often yield information or subject's whereabouts.

12. Subject discovers investigator:

    (a) If an investigator is recognized by the subject as a surveillance agent, he should normally drop out and be replaced by another investigator.
    (b) In some cases where concealment of any investigative activity is paramount, surveillance should be stopped as soon as the subject is believed to suspect surveillance.

13. Decoys:

    (a) A clever subject who has discovered that he is under surveillance may not reveal his discovery but may attempt to "shake" them from his trail by means of false contacts or decoys.
    (b) For example, a subject may leave a briefcase or package full of worthless papers or materials with a contact and thus cause unwary investigators to redirect or discontinue their surveillance, thus leaving him free to make his real contacts unobserved.

14. Traps:

    (a) A subject may attempt to lure an investigator into a trap.
    (b) A thorough knowledge of the area, combined with good judgment and the alertness to realize when trailing becomes suspiciously easy, is a good defense against traps.

Detection of foot surveillance. Common methods used by suspects to test for surveillance:

1. Stopping abruptly and looking behind for people.
2. Casually looking around.
3. Reversing course and retracing steps.
4. Boarding buses and alighting just before they start.
5. Riding short distances on buses.
6. Circling the block in a taxi.
7. Entering a building and leaving immediately via another exit.
8. Stopping abruptly after turning a corner.
9. Using convoys.
10. Watching reflections in shop windows.
11. Walking slowly and rapidly at alternate intervals.
12. Dropping a piece of paper to see if anyone retrieves it.
13. Stopping to tie shoestring while looking around for surveillance investigators.
14. Arranging with a friend in a shop, tavern or other places to watch for investigator.
15. Observing from a window or roof across street with binoculars to see if equipment or persons are visible in rooms adjacent to subject's room.
16. In hotel lobbies and similar places, watching for persons peeking over or around newspapers and watching in wall mirrors to see who is unusually observant of persons coming and going through the lobby.
17. Starting to leave a hotel lobby or similar place quickly, then suddenly turning around to see if anyone has suddenly jumped up without any apparent reason or objective.
18. The subject or an associate may attempt to be near enough to hall doors or rooms adjacent to his in order to get a quick look inside when someone happens to open the room door.
19. Subject may open and close his hotel room door to indicate that he has left the room, then wait inside the room with the door ajar. If anyone leaves an adjoining room, the subject then actually leaves his room in an ordinary manner and rides down the elevator with his neighbor while committing his appearance to memory.
20. Subject may pretend to leave his hotel room but remain quiet for awhile to see if typing, talking or other noises begin to occur in an adjoining room, indicating a possible surveillance. He then may make his presence in the room known to see if the typing suddenly stops or if the talking changes to whispers.

Eluding foot surveillance. Common methods used to lose investigators:

1. Jumping off a bus or subway just as the doors are about to close.
2. Leaving a building through the rear or side exit.
3. Losing one's self in crowds.
4. Entering theaters and leaving immediately through an exit.
5. Pointing out the investigator to a policeman, who will generally require the investigator to explain his actions.
6. Using decoys.
7. Using traps, e.g., the subject may leave a note in a phone booth, trash can or other location and then look back to see if someone is reading the note. The subject may also detect an investigator by leading him into a blind alley or hallway.
8. Taking the last taxi at a stand.
9. Changing clothing.

Automobile Surveillance

The "primary" vehicle. During surveillance, the vehicle that is the closest to or immediately behind the subject vehicle will generally act as the "primary" vehicle, and as such will radio/phone directions and information to the other cars. The primary position will change from one car to another during the surveillance. Radio/cell phone transmissions must be as short and concise as possible, giving accurate and essential information. All investigators should use the radio/cell phone only to acknowledge orders or give essential information. This will reduce the possibility of two or more vehicles transmitting at the same time.

Beginning the surveillance operation. Usually the surveillance operation will begin in the area where the subject vehicle is parked. The primary vehicle should be in a position from which the subject vehicle can be viewed with the other cars deployed strategically in the area covering anticipated routes of travel. As the subject drives away, the primary investigator will direct the most appropriate car to assume the position and the other cars to take positions at the rear or on a paralleling course. The subject will be more likely to check for a "tail" at the beginning of his trip and when near his destination than at any other time. Therefore, the investigators must be especially careful at these times.

Distance between subject and surveillance automobiles. During the surveillance, the primary car must use every means possible to avoid a prolonged appearance within the rear view vision of the subject. This may be done by keeping one or two unrelated vehicles between the subject and the primary car.

It should also be kept in mind that most people are not as observant as we are prone to give them credit for being. It can be just as easy to break off surveillance for a mistaken perception of being "made," as it is to be "made" by following too closely. When you have multiple surveillance vehicles, use the opportunity to rotate vehicles so that neither of these is likely to happen. There should rarely be the need for any one investigator to be strictly designated as a lead surveillance vehicle.

As was stated earlier, the basic concepts of what the investigator should do when difficulties are encountered on a foot surveillance should be applied with mobile surveillance. The frame of mind or thought patterns should be the same for both of these types of surveillance, and so, except for the obvious differences in what can be done from one to the next, your reactions to difficulties that you encounter should be much the same.

A brief word on stationary surveillance. Stationary surveillance, which will be most frequently encountered by entry level investigators when performing workers' compensation claim fraud investigations, presents different challenges. They are, in general, easier to address in a preventative fashion. Almost all of them can be addressed under the general category of *advance work*.

Advance work is just what it sounds like: going out to the surveillance location a week or more ahead of time to determine the best surveillance position that will provide maximum observation potential with minimal detection risk; determining what the typical traffic patterns are in the immediate and surrounding area; determining if the subject has a designated parking space; determining if the subject has a particular office/space/or area inside the location; and, asking the client as many questions as you can think to ask about the subject so that you have as much information as possible to work with.

Lastly, ensure you, your vehicle, and your related equipment are able to remain stationary for extended periods. Check batteries and their related power sources. You may not be able to address bathroom issues from four to twelve to twenty-four hours. Is your vehicle equipped to address that issue? Is your vehicle equipped to address weather-related issues (extreme heat, cold, humidity)? Most of these and similar issues can be addressed by relatively inexpensive and undetectable alterations to the typical mini-van or SUV. Knowing whether or not you can be relatively motionless in a confined space for an extended period of time, is a question only you can answer.

 Checking in with law enforcement. Unless otherwise directed by a supervisor, always check in with law enforcement prior to conducting a stationary, and particularly an extensive stationary, surveillance investigation. The majority of times, you will be in the back of a van or large sport utility vehicle. Being a good surveillance investigator, you will have arrived early, and your vehicle will have a combination of tinting and drapes so that no one will know you are back there. On the other hand, your vehicle, which none of the curious, suspicious, and perhaps nosy neighbors recognize, may be reported to the police. If you haven't checked in, law enforcement *will* drive out to your location, and they will be able to determine that you're back there, and they will ask you to step out and identify yourself. Will you get in any real trouble? Not likely, but you'll probably at least get lectured. Will they chase you out? Not likely, but they could. **More importantly**, everyone in the neighborhood, including the subject of your surveillance, will soon know you were there in the back of the van.

 Checking in requires that you provide information about yourself and any other investigators who might be out on the assignment. You will need to provide a description of your vehicle, as well as those of any other investigators. You will need to provide an approximate time frame you will be out there (hours, and number of days where applicable). You do not need to identify the client or the nature of the investigation (except where it obviously makes sense—criminal investigations, etc.). If you're an entry level investigator being given an assignment, don't hesitate to ask about checking in with law enforcement. Larger surveillance agencies may have people in the office who do all of the advance work, including checking in with law enforcement. But, with advance work in general, and especially with respect to checking in with law enforcement, always ask, always be sure.

CHAPTER SIX

Undercover Operations

Undercover operations at the entry level are typically the placement of an investigator within the client's company as a regular employee to observe the *normal* activities of employees. Although there are other instances where undercover operations are performed, for the entry level investigator, this is what the experience is likely to be.

Although many private detectives would argue this with me, a large aspect of being a successful undercover operative is being an objectively observant actor/actress. From assignment to assignment, whether you alter identities or perfect a particular one, you will need to maintain your cover identity at all times that you are involved with company personnel, and while this can be fun, it can also be difficult. Those people that you would normally be known to associate with will most likely be the types of persons you cannot afford to associate with. Often times, people you do "get tight with" will be people who are terminated and/or arrested. And, most importantly, maintaining your real identity does not have to become a difficulty. Despite what a lot of people might tell you, it is possible to be an effective undercover operative who appears to be an undesirable when appropriate and remains a respectable professional outside those particular circumstances. So, when you hear well-known actors and actresses talking about the difficulty in their work, think about the fact that an undercover operative must do the same job of acting. In addition, they must do the work that is actually required by someone in that position at the client company and report on all their senses perceive throughout the day.

For those not yet in the field, there are certain practical steps that can be taken if you are determined to work undercover. First, obtain a P.O. box. Each time you are assigned to an undercover, you will have to go through the normal hiring procedures for that client company, and you do not want to list a real address. A P.O. box is often your best alternative because you can avoid questions about the neighborhood or at least a specific address in relation to a neighborhood. Putting down a false address can lead to questions about the area, and/or someone attempting to verify that you in fact live at that address. Client companies will do their best to maintain security over personnel files, and the agents will be removed when the investigation is terminated. To the best of your ability, however, prepare for contingencies. If the unlikely does happen and a suspicious person looks at your file, having your post office box address will not get them far.

What cannot be stressed too much about the undercover operations within the field of private investigations is that, as an operative, you have to keep the job. Most people are unsuccessful operatives either because they do not take report writing seriously or because they have no work ethic. Whether you are working at a factory, warehouse, or a cruise line, you are responsible for working as hard as anyone else would have to work in order to maintain a position in the company. At most, two people within the company will know your true identity. Those people will most often be the President or Owner and the Director of Human Resources. Your immediate supervisor at the client company and all other management/supervisory staff will know you only as another employee and so will expect an honest day's work from you. You can be fired by these people. You must convince these people, as well as your fellow workers, that you need to this job by showing up for work on time and on a daily basis. It is perfectly acceptable to be a disgruntled worker if that fits within the context of that particular operation. The one way you never want to be known is a "goody-two-shoes" or "ass-kisser." Remember, you must retain the position by the same standards as any other worker.

As was stated earlier, the undercover operative must be capable of acting or portraying the personality of an "undesirable." Acting and reporting are the two primary investigative duties involved with undercover operations. But, also you know going in those are the investigative duties. Being able to do the work is of primary importance. These are rarely glamorous positions. Occasionally, they will not be blue collar, but to a larger degree, they are. To become an effective undercover operative, you will often be coordinating with law enforcement, so it is also important that you maintain a level of professionalism. That is, once you are away from the client company, you are no longer the "undesirable".

As a final introductory note, remember that the client company will want to know about all violations of company policy, from sexual harassment to the use of narcotics, from racial problems to theft problems, from safety violations to time-card fraud. They will want to know especially about any supervisory or management staff involved with any of these activities. Your client needs to know because these people have the ability to exert influence over everyone that works under them.

Your reports should reflect all observations about all persons you encounter or observe. Your reports are your end product and, therefore, should reflect all information that you have been able to obtain. Remember, the client has hired you to help them make their facility a better place to work, as well as to determine if there are persons engaged in activities that violate company policy or the law. Any smart businessman will know that, if his workers are satisfied with their positions, there is a little likelihood of theft or other problems that result primarily from having disgruntled employees.

As one last service to your client, as well as yourself, determine if they will be having future employees screened. If not, inform them of the services that you offer. You can also refer them to companies that do offer the services you aren't able to provide.

Receiving the assignment. The supervisor at any detective agency you are working for is responsible for discussing the operation to which you are assigned. This discussion should be very detailed. It is essential that you fully understand that assignment and what is expected. It is your responsibility, however, to ensure you are sufficiently informed to accept the assignment; if there are questions you have and do not ask, you have only yourself to blame. In all areas of investigations, common sense should be your guide, and common sense will tell you that a supervisor is only human and is, therefore, capable of mistakes or lapses. Speaking from experience, a supervisor who doesn't welcome questions is one who isn't concerned about you or the client.

Proper preparation is the key to success. There are several important considerations necessary to get off to a good start. The following list is provided to assist. Use this list as a general guideline, and if a supervisor fails to brief you on any of these points, be sure to raise the issue yourself.

1. Determine the client's specific problem(s).
2. Determine the time and place to apply for the position in the client's firm.
3. Determine what job (title) you should be applying for.
4. Determine if the person who will interview you at the client's location is aware of your true identity.
5. Determine if the client's employment office will check your background and, if so, work out an acceptable background with your supervisor, one that will stand up to inquiry. Background includes business, personal references, and education level.
6. Determine your pay—what will you receive from the client and from your company?
7. Determine what expenses are authorized for this assignment. This includes time and expenses for cultivation of employees after working hours.
8. Determine the clothing to be worn when applying for the position. Determine if special clothing/equipment is required for the position itself.
9. Determine how you will contact your investigative supervisor during day and evening hours.
10. Determine who you will call if your investigative supervisor cannot be reached.
11. Turn over all detective agency identification to your supervisor.
12. Determine when and how often you are to contact your investigative supervisor while on this assignment.

Reporting on employees' activities while on their own time is not acceptable. While it is normal to cultivate employees' trust by associating with them outside the client's business, it is not acceptable to write reports on the activities while doing so. Individuals who are terminated due to information obtained about them while away from the company have proven grounds for a lawsuit. Your objective in "cultivation" or "roping" should always be to establish a closer association with possible suspects so that this association will make them comfortable with you. Then, hopefully, if these suspects are engaged in any activities while at work, they will inform you of them and invite you to participate.

When developing your pretext background, remember to apply common sense. Whatever you choose to tell anyone about your education, employment history, time in the military, etc. should be something you are actually familiar with, either through your own experience or through contacts. Whatever you tell one employee once you have started in the position, you need to tell everyone you come in contact with. **Do not portray yourself as such as lowlife that people will question how you obtained the position. Also, do not speak of that which you know not.** If you were in the service, use that as a source of common ground for conversation. If you never in the service, do not attempt to pretend that you were, unless you have sufficient knowledge from research or contacts. If fishing is a hobby, determine if that can be utilized. Within the last three years, we have found that a large percentage of undesirable employees are heavily into video games. Remember, again, in investigations in general, and especially in undercovers, there is no such thing as useless knowledge, only knowledge that is not put to appropriate use.

As regards "street" knowledge, there are certain types that can be learned. Narcotics terminology, prices, and weights can be learned by training, as can similar terminology about theft and other activities. Obtaining "street smarts" is something that, generally speaking, only comes with time. Learning various cultural-specific knowledge can only come from encountering that culture. But, more and more, law enforcement and private detective personnel are offering these types of knowledge through training. These are tips, hints, and insight. Common sense cannot be taught.

Remember also that your pretext background should not be one that draws attention to you. Rather, it should be one that appears to keep you as close to average as possible. If you appear too "dirty," personnel will be afraid to associate with you. A history of arrests is not unusual, but a history of convictions will paint you as either incompetent to street-wise personnel or scary. If you are too "clean," you could be a snitch, boss's cousin, or similar undesirable in the eyes of the violators. Keep in mind that some supervisory or management-level personnel may be involved with the problem activities, and, therefore, they must also believe your pretext background.

The essential rule is that your pretext background should be one that you are comfortable with. Your new identity must be one you can convince yourself of as much as others. No, this does not mean schizophrenia. This means you should be able to answer suspects' follow-up questions about parts of your background. It means that you must be confident that you could receive an Emmy or an Oscar for your performance.

Applying for the Position. Essential to applying for the job is remembering that your investigative assignment has already begun. You must be "in character" at this time, and you must be an observant investigator. This should be the point at which you begin to collect information for reports and that you begin to present your pretext personality. Be polite and professional, as if you were actually nervous about obtaining the position, but take advantage of opportunities to add some color to your personality. For instance, if asked whether or not you can pass a drug screening, you could say, "I got it covered," or, "I don't worry about the tests," instead of just answering "yes." These answers leave room for doubt, without making a definite statement. As always, remember to evaluate the individuals you are in contact with when making these decisions. You are the person out in the field; therefore, only you can decide what is appropriate.

Arrive at the client's employment office on time or early if possible. Appearing anxious to obtain the position is almost always a recommended part of your pretext. People will need to perceive you as someone who needs this opportunity.

Inquire about the position in the manner previously discussed with your investigative supervisor. Unless circumstances at the location dictate otherwise, do not deviate from what your investigative supervisor has informed you to do. Your supervisor will have previously determined what is the most appropriate approach. If the person at the location tells you something contradictory, follow that person's instructions, and, immediately after departing the area, contact your investigative supervisor.

If the receptionist informs you that the company is not hiring, request to fill out an application for future reference. Again, immediately after departing the area, contact your investigative supervisor.

Caution: If the person interviewing you is aware of your true identity and asks any questions in regards to your investigative employment or other assignments you were on, simply reply that regulations forbid your discussing it. Do not be influenced by their persuasive attempts to get your to talk. You are not allowed to discuss company matters with them, ever.

Ascertain the date and time you are to report for work. Determine what your rate of pay and hours will be. To the best of your ability, determine if there is any regular overtime, if there is a training or probationary period initially, and if the company is accepting applications for various positions or just one.

Then, after departing the area, begin your report-writing immediately. Describe the persons you observed, report on the efficiency of the department, and indicate how the applicant is treated. If drug-screening was part of that application process, report on the screening procedure (i.e., how many forms of identification were you asked to produce, were you watched while filling the sample bottle, etc.). If the drug screen is done on a later date, or at a different facility, write a separate report.

Areas of Investigation. Most companies will hire your agency for what is known as a general survey investigation. That is, they will want to know about all areas of their operation that need attention or improvement. Safety is the primary concern, and production is the secondary. Of the areas listed below, most are of concern because of a direct relation to safety at the client facility. Theft, although of monetary concern to the client, is also a safety concern for the consumer.

Drugs, narcotics, and alcohol. For obvious reasons, the client will be concerned as to whether or not employees are under the influence of any of these substances. Safety is one of the not-so-often thought of reasons. Ask yourself, do you want someone under the influence of alcohol or controlled substances driving a forklift? Operating machinery? Working with tools? Controlling an assembly or other production line? Being responsible for inventories? And, in regard to the distribution of controlled substances on company property, the company has every right to worry. Again, ask yourself: do you want to be shot by a stray bullet from a deal gone wrong? Do you want to witness an overdose or reaction to "doctored" drugs? For those operatives who encounter controlled substances at the workplace, there are rules to follow and knowledge to obtain.

First, remember that you should always be coordinating to some degree with local law enforcement. Your investigative supervisor should be establishing those contacts as the need arises. Second, unless told otherwise by your investigative supervisor, **do not** transport any controlled substances outside the client company. Third, do not discuss any transactions with anyone but your investigative supervisor. The client's need-to-know basis will be determined by your investigative supervisor. Last, but far from least, do not use any controlled substances unless you have a reasonable belief that there is the imminent threat of death or great bodily harm if you do not do so. Also, your reports in regards to all activities related to these subject matters need special attention to detail. It may never happen, but the possibility exists that you will be required to testify in a court of law or at other proceedings.

A last word on this subject, and one that applies to all types of activity that the company is interested in discovering. **Entrapment** is the word the investigator needs to keep in mind at all times. **Do not** be the person to initiate conversations that directly address behavior that is contradictory to company policy, the law, or safety. **Do not** encourage personnel to engage in any acts that are unsafe or contradictory to company policy. **Do not** request personnel to engage in activities that they were not doing for others previously. Remember that your responsibility is initially to observe, become involved at the point at that you have determined that, in fact, certain personnel are engaged in these activities, and document each occasion that you are involved with or observe these activities taking place.

Theft. Theft is one of the more common thoughts that come to mind in regards to undercover operations. As an investigator, these are several things to keep in mind, both in regards to types of theft and the various methods utilized to perpetrate them. A general thought to bear in mind on this subject as well as others is that you need to think like the violator. You need to remember why someone is stealing so that you can establish a pretext story that gives you similar reasons, and you need to project the image of someone who would be capable of doing so. Almost every company or corporation suffers from some form of theft, and where substance abuse is present, for instance, there is a good likelihood the users are committing the theft to support a habit too expensive to fit within the budget after bills are paid for their wages.

Types of theft range from time card fraud to large scale removal of company product. What is important to remember is that separately, or combined, these different types of theft can cost the company literally millions. For each incident where someone punches in for someone who is not present or who does not appear until later, the company not only loses moneys in terms of wages but also in terms of production. Each type of theft needs to be reported on, and each report must be factual and accurate no matter the type. Of course, the wholesale theft of company product will be more difficult to detect initially. Your investigative supervisor should recognize and allow for the fact that more time will be required to establish this type of theft. But, there are certain standard methods.

One of these methods is commonly referred to as "trash removal day". Perfectly good product will be placed into garbage receptacles on the outside of the facility, and either the workers themselves or their contacts will retrieve that product from the trash after business hours.

Another method is that workers will establish a contact with an outside distribution company, and when a truck arrives to pick up six skids of product, the truck will receive seven. Both the shipping person from the company and the driver from the company will of course sign the inventory sheet that reflects six skids. The seventh will be dropped off at an agreed upon location, and the product will most likely find its way to a flea market, Maxwell street, or even a small store.

Another common method is the simple "pocketing" of small, but valuable, product. While this might not seem very profitable in direct relation to the risk, there are several things to remember. First, over time anyone could use this method to increase his or her income if the individual product is expensive. Secondly, a percentage of personnel will do this simply to supplement their income so that they can afford other nasty habits.

Some of the simple indicators of possible suspect personnel are personnel who live beyond their apparent means. Personnel who are "stylin" even though they shouldn't be able to afford to do so. This is where paying attention to people's shoes can be important. If someone is only making five-fifty an hour but wears different pairs of Nike pumps, the latest "grunge" fashions, or has excessive jewelry, there is a good chance these were purchased with moneys gained through illegal activities to support their illegal habit.

Greed is another important word for the investigator to remember. Being careful to avoid entrapment, the investigator should attempt to determine suspects and then, through indirect reference (suggestions in casual conversation that the investigator could probably "get rid of" some product through outside personnel), attempt to present those people with an opportunity to tell you about how they can get the product out. Often times, these personnel will be employees who have been with the company for a significant period of time. They will have an established method and group of clients for the product and so have little reason to allow outsiders in. But greed, revenge, and perversity remain the three main motivations for criminal activity.

Morale is a good indicator of the likelihood that theft is occurring at the client facility. Although most people would not consider this the subject of an undercover, it is a concern that clients wish reflected in their reports. The morale of employees will greatly affect productivity and the likelihood that other problems exist. If a client's workers are generally disgruntled, the undercover investigator's responsibility is to attempt to determine the origin of the unhappiness.

Monetary compensation will be a factor, but it is not often that this is the sole reason for low morale. Supervisory and management personnel should be considered as "suspects" who are at least partially responsible for a low level of morale. Company policies will dictate, but the enforcement, or lack thereof, is a primary responsibility of supervisory and management personnel. If enforcement is seen as indiscriminate or used to discriminate against particular individuals or groups, this needs to be noted. The presence of racial, sexual, or other types of harassment will often be indicative of poor supervisory or management staff.

Favoritism on the part of anyone with a position of authority will result in poor morale. Workers are made to feel as if hard work will not necessarily be rewarded appropriately, and therefore motivation will suffer.

If employees do not feel that they have some type of voice within the company and that they can in fact influence their own circumstances, this will cause morale to suffer. Employees need to have an outlet for their complaints and some ability to make suggestions. Whether it is through the appointment of personnel to represent them in meetings, or set meetings between management and personnel, this is an issue that needs to be addressed. And, for the undercover investigator, part of your responsibility is to attempt to determine and recommend a course of action for the client.

Harassment. Because there are different groups that are sometimes subject to harassment, the subject will be covered in general as opposed to each specific group. Harassment can take different forms in relation to the different groups but is generally a matter that is observed or overheard. The undercover investigator must most importantly remember a basic lesson to investigators in general—document, document, document.

Verbal harassment can come from any level of person in relation to the victim. It should be noted that all incidents need to be reported, as each is likely to have a similar effect. In one particular investigation, I observed an instance in which an individual was being harassed by other workers because of his association with members who did not belong to the same group as those people who were harassing him. Verbal harassment can have an emotional and psychological effect on the victim and can affect the morale of many people. Although it is more difficult for companies to address the issue of verbal harassment, most will want to know about this. Having the word of a trained, objective investigator in regards to incidents will help to establish the reality of the situation and the particular circumstances.

If harassment escalates from verbal to physical, the investigators observations of both become even more invaluable. Whether or not an incident was actually precipitated by an exchange of words is in itself important. There may be times when an individual is simply assaulted in one way or another with no conflict developing immediately prior to the incident. These ambushes require "the right place at the right time," but, on the other hand, by substantiating the previous incidents whenever possible, the investigator can help to establish what is the version of the story most likely to be accurate. In your reports, however, **do not deduce, guess, or offer opinion.** Reports are for facts only. Deductions and opinions of the investigator are to remain in the verbal arena, unless directed to do otherwise by your investigative supervisor.

And, in regards to physical contact, remember to describe all types of physical contact as accurately as possible. It is not only a punch or kick that denotes noteworthy contact. Also, describe the reaction on the part of the individual who is the subject of physical contact. Some victims, though hurt, disturbed or disgusted, might choose not to report what others have reported for fear of losing their position or being ostracized by fellow workers.

Safety. This is not often thought of as the responsibility of the undercover investigator. From unsafe acts of employees to safety hazards present within the facility, remember to report these. And, whenever possible, attempt to determine if a supervisory or management level person was aware of the problem. Companies do want to know if those persons are doing the job they are getting paid extra money for.

As regards safety, remember that the use of drugs or alcohol is an important matter. Issues of distribution and the criminal offense even of possession aside, if someone is responsible for driving a forklift, running a production line, or working with tools and machinery, drugs will influence their ability to do so, as will alcohol.

Horseplay needs to be kept in check where appropriate. Obviously the investigator needs to determine by a period of time what an acceptable level of horseplay is, but, as a general guideline, so they are most likely a good gauge.

The general rule to reporting safety hazards for the undercover investigator is that if the hazard is immediate, bring it to someone's attention, if not necessarily a manager. By allowing a worker with more time in to report it to the supervisor, you have accomplished at least two things; you have deferred to that worker, thereby boosting his or her ego, and you have shown yourself as someone who does not like to speak with supervisors or managers. If immediate action is required in regards to the imminent risk of injury, take that action and then report the situation as appropriate to the particular circumstances. Do not risk jeopardizing your pretext by telling anyone of any training you have received. Do what is necessary and give only necessary information if questioned by anyone about the incident.

For the undercover investigator, all of the listed areas need attention, consideration, and documentation. It is part of what makes the assignment a challenge. Having to maintain your position within the company by performing the duties of the position and being subject to the same rules as other employees is the complicating factor. Poor report-writing and a poor work ethic are the main reasons that most investigators, though competent in other areas, cannot effectively operate an undercover assignment. And, do not be mistaken, you will encounter other investigators and critics who will discredit the work the undercover investigator does. As I myself have heard from various persons in and outside the industry, "well, it takes more than dressing like a rag-bag to be a private investigator." They are quite right. And, while they straighten their ties, comb their moussed hair, and shuffle their papers, I reply that it takes much more, especially to be an undercover operative responsible for putting in a day's work and a day's investigation.

Performing the Assignment. Performing the undercover assignment requires quite a lot of effort and attention to detail from the investigator. The effort is directly related to going to a dull job every day. Getting up early, or going in on a swing shift, you will be subject to the schedule of the average working class American. Attention to detail is a basic rule for investigators' in any assignment, but, for the undercover investigator, it means learning the position as well as being an actor/actress, being a trained observer, and a report-writer. This chapter will address issues related to actually performing the assignment.

Reporting to work. As often as is possible without drawing attention to yourself, report early for work, in the range of fifteen minutes to half an hour. Develop a reasonable explanation for this if you can do this on a regular basis. Being subject to public transportation in the city of Chicago is a built in excuse for not being able to rely upon arrival time. And, for people with their own transportation, another unintended assist is that, as far as driving, there are only two seasons in the Chicago Metro area: winter and road construction. Use your imagination. If you're telling people that you're married, tell anyone that might be curious about your early arrival about wanting to get away from the ball and chain. As long as it is believable, it is acceptable. Again, creativity balanced by common sense.

While actually engaged in the work of your position, do not appear to be overly eager to please. Initially, for the first two weeks, it is acceptable to prove that you can do the work necessary to maintain the position, and if that requires an eager approach, then adopt the attitude of someone who needs the work. If the position itself does not require concentration, motivation, and a great deal of effort, however, only put forth that effort necessary to retain the position. Do your regular job at a pace relative to your fellow employees. **Do not call attention to yourself by either high or low production.** Take the same time for lunch and coffee breaks as the other employees.

Working throughout the day. As was stated, take the same amount of time for lunch and breaks as appears to be the average. Pay attention, and learn if there is an acceptable lee-way in regards to time allotted for lunch and breaks. In regards to being eager to please supervisors, remember that you should not appear to be someone even capable of considering career involvement with an organization. Within the context of staying on a supervisor's "good side," some extra effort is acceptable, as long as it does not cross over into the realm of the "brown-noser," "suck-up," or "kiss-up." And, before I forget to mention this again, remember that most of what is written is general guidelines. As the investigator at the assignment, there are always certain judgment calls you will have to make. In regards to these judgment calls, the most important question to ask yourself is, "what will most assist me in achieving the objective of the assignment?" Volunteering for additional or more difficult assignments is generally not a good idea, unless there is reason to believe that it would allow you to get close with an individual who is considered a suspect person. Working overtime needs to be cleared prior to accepting the assignment. Generally speaking, accepting overtime hours is recommended. It assists in the appearance that you are in need of more money and can allow for quicker cultivation of employees. Often companies will have a "Saturday crew" conduct their overtime on Saturdays. This will often mean that all or most of the supervisory and management staff will not be present, and it therefore will be a good opportunity to take advantage of. In most instances, you will find that what is said and done at an organization when there is not supervisory presence is distinctly different from what occurs under more normal circumstances. And, in regards to theft, there is always a greater likelihood that thieves will operate when there is a lessened presence of authority figures.

Cultivation, or roping, of employees. The basic rule for cultivation of employees is as follows: do so whenever possible, remembering to remain within the realistic restrictions of your pretext. Any conversations conducted between you and other employees are opportunities to learn. Listening is an extremely important part of communication, and for the undercover investigator, listening has an additional benefit. Whether engaged in conversation, or merely overhearing conversations that take place, pay attention. Any information that you can obtain can serve the purpose of assisting you in cultivating employees. If it is not necessarily noteworthy in the sense that it should be put into your report, it may, on the other hand, allow you to develop common ground to approach conversations with. Knowing what people think of anything from supervisory personnel to politics to baseball can assist you in establishing common grounds for conversation. Always remember to stay within the limitations of your pretext and never give out conflicting information unless it fits within your pretext. Generally speaking, however, it is not recommended to be known as a storyteller or liar as part of your pretext identity; that reputation will most likely inhibit your ability to "get tight" with people.

Cultivation of employees will begin as soon as the job does, but, within the first week you should not press. Do not appear to be over-eager to make new friends. Be receptive, but not necessarily out-going. Here again, you must be the one to make the judgment calls based upon the disposition of fellow employees. If an overall friendly atmosphere is present, then assimilate yourself appropriately. The bottom line being that presenting oneself as an average employee is the best objective.

There are certain restrictions involved with the cultivation of employees, and they need to be strictly followed. If you should opt to ignore these warnings, be prepared for civil lawsuits, loss of employment, and a reputation that will follow you throughout your career.

- **Do not suggest to an employee of the client's firm that they commit an irregularity.** Whether against policy, against OSHO regulations, or against the law, entrapment is a reasonable defense that will apply under all circumstances. Entrapment does not apply only in regards to criminal actions. A professional, ethical investigator would not suggest to an employee to commit and irregularity anyway; if conducting an undercover operation properly, you will be able to observe infractions of any nature eventually.

    If engaged in cultivating activities outside the client's company location, your objective needs to be gaining closer association to employees. Unless at company-sponsored or organized activities (bowling league, softball team, etc.), reports will be necessary only as directed by your investigative supervisor. Again, common sense applies here. If conversation and/or activities do not directly relate back to the company, the investigator does not report on those conversations or activities. And, because talk is cheap, take subjects of conversation with a grain of salt. If employees are discussing ways to steal from the company or similar subjects, make a report/notes for yourself for purpose of documentation, and then, if there are actually any actions taken by those employees, your investigative supervisor can consult with an attorney as to whether or not those reports/notes can be utilized to any degree.

- **Do not report either in verbal or written form on lawful union activities, members, meetings, etc.** This includes any information concerning individuals attempting to organize a union at the client's location. You are not to report on an employee's pro or con union position. At certain assignments it may be necessary for you to join a union after a certain period of employment; however, this does not authorize you to report on any of the union activities either in writing or verbally. You are forbidden to report on any such matters because of certain provisions of the Wagner Act.

A final word in regard to the cultivation of employees: patience. Cultivation of employees is one of your most effective means of resolving problems. However, people who are involved with theft, drugs, or other activities have a suspicious nature and something they feel is worth protecting. They are not going to immediately or freely distribute information. Developing various aspects of your pretext should be done so with this thought in mind. Making these people believe they have something to gain by involving you in their activities will increase the likelihood that they will do just that. Remember, greed is a primary motivator. Patience will prove the difference between a professional and otherwise.

Try not to be absent from work, unless it is absolutely necessary. The day that you are not present may be the day you could have gotten the break that solves the client's problem. Maintaining a proper pretext includes behaving as if you need this position. So, even more than the average employee, you cannot afford to be absent.

When an absence is necessary, adhere to the client's employment policies regarding absences. Promptly call your immediate supervisor at the client's business and/or the persons who are normally notified, and inform them of your reason for absence and when you will return. Immediately after doing so, notify your investigative supervisor.

As a final note to this chapter, remember also that your paycheck being correct and on time is dependent upon you. Reports, time and expense forms should be mailed or brought to your investigative supervisor regularly. Often, it will be best to mail reports. Your investigative supervisor will advise you. Taking the chance that someone at the client's company will observe you on the outside is always a possibility for serious consideration.

Reporting. Your initial report will be in regards to applying for the position and should be written in the third person, as should all reports. This report should contain all the information that was obtained in regards to the logistics (pay rate, hours, etc.) of the position that you will occupy at the client company. Also included should be information in regards to any tests that were given, including results and manner of administration, the results of any physical examinations, an evaluation of the thoroughness of those examinations; and a general, overall review of the application process, efficiency and attitude of personnel.

First week. Your primary responsibility during the first week of your assignment involves three aspects to consider. First, familiarize yourself with the requirements of your position at the client's company. Next, acquaint yourself with those employees of your position at the client's company and those employees you will be working with. The third consideration is to become familiar with the physical layout of the business.

Familiarizing yourself with the requirement of your position will vary in difficulty according to assignment. Remember, as a professional undercover operative you must first concentrate on becoming an employee of the client's company. And, for the purposes of reporting, you must remember the instructions you received on your duties and who has those instructions. Being a new employee, it is likely that you will encounter various personnel who will assign you different responsibilities; to the best of your ability report on each. Report on the actual assignment, the individuals giving them, and the manner/attitude of those individuals. Supervisors should introduce themselves, but if they do not, describe them as accurately as possible. And remember, an investigator **should** be a trained observer and, therefore, **should** use all of their senses to obtain information. Someone, for instance, will probably call out the name(s) of your supervisors and fellow workers.

Second week. Describe those employees who names you do not learn, reporting the relative competency of fellow employees and how you were greeted by them. Attempt to determine the area where each employee parks his or her vehicle. And, if there are any blatant violations of company policy or the law, that will need to be included in your report. Be friendly to all, but concentrate on doing your job. Keep in mind what you are there for and that you need to work carefully and efficiently toward obtaining that objective.

Becoming familiar with the physical lay-out of the client company's facility is another matter that should be done with a careful approach. If your position within the company is one that initially limits your mobility, confining you to a specific area under direct supervision, then work within those limitations. Take your time to get to know the position, and by adapting you will eventually determine the available opportunities to step outside those restrictions. If being able to move freely takes three weeks, then, as long as you have been documenting your limitations with your report, that should not present a problem with the client. Included with your reports and related to attempting to learn the lay-out should be the condition of your work area and those areas you normally come across. Where employees normally eat, smoke, and take breaks may have a direct relation to various violations. This information will all prove important down the line.

Third week. During the third week of your assignment, your reports should no longer emphasize the daily routine. You should already have established that through the reports of your first and second week. Your primary focus should now be the cultivation of employees, and your reports should reflect that. Even during your second week, you should not be over-eager to make new friends, but if the opportunity to engage in after work activity presents itself, take advantage of it. Remember to review this undercover guide more frequently as you begin to develop your assignment—it will keep you from getting into any legal trouble, and it will keep your reports from becoming repetitions of general knowledge. Your mobility should be slightly improved, and your familiarity with fellow-workers should also begin to develop. But, do not take this as a fixed schedule—remember you are making the judgment calls. Do not press on any matters and especially not on theft or drugs. People who are anxious to become involved with theft or drugs will be considered one of two things: not street smart or a narc. And those people who are involved with either of those activities on a regular basis will not have any desire to be associated with you. Remember, as a final general operating rule and one that is very important, allow other persons to approach you on subjects regarding violations of company policy and/or the law, initially be hesitant to become involved (play it off that you need the job and that you can't afford to get in trouble; in other words, play if off in a manner that is most appropriate to your pretext), and then later, you will most likely have another opportunity to accept their offer for involvement.

At the back of this text is an index of questions related to the various areas that you, as an undercover operative, need to be concerned with. These questions will assist you in determining directions, and various approaches. Review this guide frequently and in particular the questions that follow. What you have already read are general operating guidelines, and some basic rules that need to be followed in order to ensure you and the investigative agency you work for stay out of legal trouble.

An undercover operative is an actor/actress, investigator, and, along with those other duties that other investigators may do, a worker. Being a successful undercover operative requires you to develop your acting skills, maintain your investigative skills, and have a strong work ethic. Not everyone can do this. And, not everyone should. Undercover operatives are not necessarily any better than other types of investigators, but don't let anyone tell you that you've got an easy job or put you down for what you do. Personally, I've worked on bank fraud cases, bail enforcement, surveillance, process service, and almost every type of investigation a private investigator will encounter except executive protection and homicide. I consider a successful undercover operative among the most versatile and useful personnel to have on board with any agency.

CASE FILES: Blue Collar Detective: The Real World of Undercover Investigations

"Hey baldy," Tom shouted from his forklift, "You don't look so hot."

"I didn't know you were looking," I replied and raised my middle finger in a familiar gesture that had become my Monday salute. "I'll remember to wear something a little tighter for you tomorrow."

"Hey Jim," Mark said, calling me over to his desk, "Got another *special project* for you."

I offered Mark my Monday salute and a *why me* look. Mark was my immediate supervisor at the company and basically a good guy. In the five months that I had been working at the company, Mark had given me two good reviews, and I had only been able to discover that he occasionally smoked marijuana on the weekends. He was a hard-working, level-headed supervisor who didn't necessarily love his job but was down to earth in his understanding that, for a high school graduate, he had worked himself to a good position with respect to pay and benefits.

"You oughta be careful," Mark said, turning down the volume of the radio on his desk. "That thing might get broken off one of these days."

"Yeah, you and what army?" I joked. Mark was six inches taller and easily forty pounds heavier, but I constantly made remarks like that to him, and it was part of the reason I had earned his respect. Hard work was the other part. He knew that if there was something that needed doing, I'd get it done. And, in the Defective Returns area of the warehouse, that was saying something. Mark was in charge of two teams in the Shipping and Receiving area, and specifically responsible for Defective Returns, which was an area that management liked to call on to complete many of their *special projects*.

Most undercover assignments only lasted three or four months, but the problems at this one had turned out to be more severe than the client had anticipated, so they had kept me on with the idea of doing as much house cleaning at once as possible. I had started working in the mailroom, which had allowed me to get to know the operation, then switched to Shipping and Receiving when I had developed suspect personnel. I had already provided the company with the information they needed to document and shut down the theft that was occurring after I left, but they also wanted to try to eliminate as much of the drug problem as they could, too. Fortunately, their President and Director of Operations understood they would also need to address morale issues related to wages, promotions and sexual harassment by one of the managers. Often with undercover operations, getting the client to understand that some employee complaints needed addressing wasn't easy.

"I know you're gonna love this one, Jim. Need to get all the one, two, and three hundred series portable units, along with their parts and miscellaneous, out of the area, into properly marked boxes and placed in the back left side of the other warehouse."

"Must be Monday," I replied and set my coffee down on his desk. "You don't mind if I breathe for a few seconds before I jump right on that?"

"No problem, baldy," Mark answered. Hey, did you check the bowling sheets? You beat Hippie up pretty bad last week."

"Only 'cuz he was askin' for it," I joked, having noticed that Hippie was coming around the corner. It wasn't until the fourth month at the company that I had been told Reggie had earned his nickname for preferring wine, marijuana, and the occasional attendance at an anti-war rally. His father had died over in Vietnam, so he was essentially against any war.

"Keep that up, Jim, I be askin' to see the Wicked Witch about racial harassment," Hippie said as he approached. "Man, way you look, you musta had a good weekend."

"Way you look, you musta seen Joan Rivers' plastic surgeon."

At a blue collar level, much like in the world of investigations and law enforcement, cutting on each other was a way of showing respect and acceptance of each other. The personal conversation that occurred at the average warehouse was almost identical to that which occurred in the average police station or investigations office. "Better watch it, Hippie," Mark said. "He's been on a roll this morning."

"Well, some of us have to work around here," I jokingly said. Hippie was Mark's Assistant Supervisor, so Tom, Benny and I always joked about the people with desks losing their sense of a work ethic. I walked to the rear of the defective returns area. I knew that today's special project was going to be a lot of work and that if I was going to be able to meet Michelle for lunch, I would have to try to get as much packing and moving done in the morning as I could. At this point in the investigation, the lunch meeting was important.

"This quarter pound isn't from the usual guy," Michelle explained as a drove down North Avenue. "I got this buddy; he's a VP at another company around here. He just needed to get rid of this; somebody paid him back a debt with this."

"As long as it's good," I lied. Purchases from people outside the company didn't do us much good, but in order to maintain a believable cover, I had to make the purchase. Of course, taking a drug test the day before and having my car searched earlier that morning was a little more annoying now, but law enforcement would still find a way to use the information. Each time you made a purchase, you were subject to a drug test before and after, your person and your vehicle being searched before and after, and being under surveillance the day of the purchase. It was all part of cooperating with law enforcement, and it was a mutually beneficial arrangement. They got leads for their investigation, and we got a little more safety.

I pulled into a parking space down from Al's, noticing the blue van parked across the street. Steve and the two narcotics officers would be ready to film the transaction from the van. When companies were interested in prosecution, we worked directly with the local police or with the Metropolitan Enforcement Group (MEG), and if they weren't interested, everything was the same, except that we didn't introduce one of their people to our source. Instead of investigations being started, people were either arrested or terminated. Typically, I was terminated or arrested at the same time, so I looked to be a victim of the undercover also.

"I wasn't really in the mood for Mexican today," Michelle said.

"Yeah, and I've had enough Mongolian beef for a few days," I replied. Al's was among the best Italian beef in Chicago. The original was located in the Little Italy neighborhood around Taylor and Morgan. That area had been where Al Capone had done a lot of business, and it was only in recent years that many of the remaining authentic Italian businesses had either expanded to new neighborhoods to stay alive, or had given way to the trendier tastes like Thai and tea shops. Al's still maintained its original location, as did Fontano's subs. A good Chicago investigator, one who had really been out on the streets, could tell you about Al's beef, Fontano's, Margie's on Cicero, and where to get the best gyro outside of Greek town. "A spicy Italian sausage with some red sauce, that's what I need."

"You're the only person I know who doesn't go to Al's for the beef," Michelle commented.

"Too easy. I'm probably the only person you know who wears a Bugs jacket too," I replied, referring to the jean jacket I was wearing. It had an embroidered picture of Bugs Bunny in an old bi-plane on the back. The jacket, along with my full beard and mustache, small hoop earring, and shoulder-length hair were all part of the look affected for blue collar undercover operations. The look was only part of it though, because, as I knew from my own youth, long hair didn't really reflect the person; it only played upon other people's assumptions.

Knowing the language, from street slang for drugs to terms particular to certain racial groups, was another part of maintaining the cover identity. The rest had to do with being regular people. Going bowling, playing softball, speaking to people at a level they understood. I had obtained a Bachelor of Arts degree with a double major in Criminal Justice and English, but using polysyllabic words in complex sentences was not going to help me fit in at the average warehouse, factory or chemical plant. And, in the real world, communicating was a matter of speaking so that you're understood, no matter whether the usage was or wasn't proper.

"You do have a definite style," Michelle replied and took a brown paper bag out of her purse, handing it over to me.

I took the two rubber bands off the bag, unrolled it, and looked inside. It was not the best *smoke* I had ever seen, nor was it the worst. Not a lot of seeds, not a lot of stems, but a little bit more to the green side. We were paying too much for it, but fortunately that was a client expense. We had to make a few purchases from Michelle, hoping that would get the word around that I was *cool*. It had taken a little longer than expected, but the end result was that I had been able to make a connection with the management level individual who was distributing *coke* and with the warehouse team leader who was distributing *smoke* (the common word for marijuana at the time). If it weren't for Michelle being too trusting, we might not have gotten anywhere though. The client had failed to mention at our initial meeting that their sister company had an undercover in a little over a year ago. Word had leaked out from their upper offices, and personnel at both companies were paranoid about narcs. Fortunately, between bowling, softball, and making a few deals with Michelle, I had gained people's confidence.

"That'll work," I said and took my wallet out of my shirt pocket. Something as simple as that, keeping your wallet in your shirt pocket instead of a pants pocket, gave people the impression you were from the city instead of the suburbs. I counted out three hundred dollars. "Freshly printed."

"Let's eat," Michelle said, stuffing the money into her purse, "I'm hungry."

After we had finished lunch, we went back to work, and I completed the laborious task of moving almost eight thousand units from one warehouse to the other. Another television myth about undercover operations. In the private sector anyway, you had to do the work, put up with the bullshit from everyone, and not get in trouble just like everyone else. In most cases, there were only one or two people who knew who you actually were, and that meant anyone who was your boss was treating you like a regular employee. It was a good lesson in humility for a lot of people in the investigations industry who thought they understood a hard day of work.

After work, I was meeting Ron, our cocaine connection, at a bar not too far from the company to purchase an *eight-ball* of cocaine. Rod had sold me a sixteenth as an initial, testing purchase. It had been fairly good coke, not heavily *stepped on* (also known as *cutting*, the term was street language for taking cocaine and mixing it with other substances to maximize profits). Two weeks later I had purchased the other eight ball. Two hundred dollars for three grams of cocaine. Women had been my cover story. I had told Ron that I never touched the stuff, but I knew a couple women who liked to party, and I had a connect in the Northwest suburbs who liked to get it from the city. That way, he could make more money selling it to the sons and daughters of the affluent, moral and decent-minded suburbanites. Rod, knowing that I had made purchases from Michelle, bought the story. He was willing to meet my guy, as long as it was away from work. That played right into what I needed to do. When we introduced an undercover law enforcement agent, we needed to do it away from the worksite, so that they could initiate their own investigation. At the time he agreed to meet, Ron probably thought he was being clever and covering his ass in case I was a company narc. He hadn't figured I would be introducing him to a MEG agent who would bust him weeks after I was out of the company.

I got out of my car, a Nissan Stanza with primer still covering the corner of the right front quarter panel. Though the dent and the repair not being completed were hardly planned, it lent itself to my cover identity, so I had not had the repair completed while I was working the undercover. The van that had been parked on North Avenue was parked a couple spots over, and as I walked toward it, one of the MEG agents walked toward my car. I would be searched in the van, while my car was searched. Some investigators resented the procedure, but it didn't bother me. It would be very easy for me to purchase a pound, report a quarter, and make a bit of money while seeming to assist law enforcement.

"Film at eleven?" I asked as the side door slid open.

"Got it real good," Dave said, motioning for me to come into the van. "Nice job counting out the money."

"Lucky for us she was stoned," I replied, watching the screen that was playing back the earlier buy from Michelle. "I think she might have been a bit uptight if she was straight."

"Let's do the drill," Dave said.

Dave searched me thoroughly. The quarter pound was still back at the warehouse, which was part of the plan. After making the introduction of Dave to Ron tonight, I would be part of a large group of employees who were either going to be terminated or put on the Employee Assistance Drug and Rehabilitation program. Employment law in Illinois, like most law, was constantly being reinterpreted and altered. In this case, employees had to be offered the opportunity for the employee assistance program when they had been found to be using drugs or alcohol while at work. People like me, who would have *accidentally* left the quarter pound in their locker when the dogs came through on an anonymous tip to the hot line at the company, would be terminated, and, in my case, arrested on outstanding warrants. It was a good way to make my disappearance not put me under suspicion as the undercover. The *arresting officers* would make it look good too: a little rough treatment and a lot of nasty remarks.

I got out of the van and walked over to the bar where I was supposed to meet Ron. Dave would show up a few minutes later, and the introduction would be made. MEG would initiate their own investigation, taking Ron down a few weeks later, and turning him into a snitch. They were not really interested in Ron beyond the fact he could take them up the ladder to his suppliers.

"Hey, Ron, how you doin'?" I joked as I walked into the bar.

Later, as I drove away from the bar, Dave and Ron getting into Ron's car was the image in my rearview mirror. I couldn't help but think about the people I had been working with. The majority were good, hard-working people. Some of them had problems, and in the eyes of the company, whether you were smoking marijuana or pounding beers, it was the same. I agreed with that because when someone is behind the wheel of a forklift or operating other factory machinery, a small mistake could be very costly. In this case in particular, I was hopeful the client realized that some of the issues concerning wages and promotions, as well as the overall work environment, needed to be addressed. Although it could be difficult to assess success or failure with an undercover in any absolute way, I had found that being able speak candidly to a client about their responsibility helped as a measure, as well as knowing that I had been able to determine the source of their immediate problem.

When you worked undercover investigations in the private sector, which were mostly at the blue collar level, you were subject to the needs and desires of the company and the restrictions of the law, so you had to find that measure of success internally. You were there working, like everyone else. Sweating, using your muscle and your mind to get the job done, eight to twelve hours a day. Then, you had to work on infiltrating the circles of people who were involved with everything from drugs, to theft, to harassment. It gave you a healthy respect for the blue collar worker and a greater appreciation for the idea of working hard and playing hard. I was counting this investigation on the success side.

CHAPTER SEVEN

Ethics and Professionalism

    Among the classes we provide, this ranks in popularity with report-writing. Why? Probably because of the limited public image provided most people via television, movies, and even books. People almost prefer to avoid the subject, hoping that by burying our heads in the sand, we can do whatever we want with the given excuse that we don't know any better. And, while I'd be the first person to admit that the best detectives have **contacts** on both sides of the legal fence, there is a world of distance between **contacts, associates, and friends.**

    Other professions have a codified version of ethics. There exists a *code of ethics* for law enforcement, attorneys, doctors, etc. Do all members of any of those professions adhere to the code of ethics? Would having a code of ethics decrease the number of professionals in our industry who cross the line? A code of ethics, while it is a good idea and might be a place to start, will not alter the identities of those people who enter the field. At best, it might deter some less desirables if it was believed that the ethical detectives would stand together to enforce such a code. And in all honesty, in the last fourteen years, about the only thing I've witnessed detectives being able to stand together about was some action on the part of government that was believed to be bad for business. Suffice it to say, at this point in time, we can only be responsible and concerned with our own actions.

    Operating ethically can probably best be defined by a simple statement: *provide excellent service at reasonable prices, and do not do that which you would not want done to yourself, family, or friends.* By reasonable rates, I do not mean to suggest that low-balling is the way to go after business. That only results in a lesser product. We are professionals and as such deserve to be paid as professionals. Going beyond this definition would probably result in another book in and of itself, if only because of the perpetual change in circumstances surrounding particular investigations. There are some obvious things that would be less than ethical (charging a client for services that were not performed, etc.), but most of those practices are either illegal, and/or, depending upon the level of regulation within your States, against the applicable Private Detective Act.

Professionalism encompasses many things, ranging from attire, to speech, to *not* slamming the competition, even if they might deserve it. It is a fairly accepted belief that the practice of slamming the competition to make yourself look better is unprofessional in any industry. Then we make ourselves look like politicians. And, as a man in a movie once said, "Hell, there ain't nothin' worse than a politician "cept maybe a child molester." Does a suit make a man? No. Should a suit be a part of your wardrobe? Yes. The truth is that while some clients might understand your work requires you to look "down and dirty" or "casual" at times, even the ones who do understand expect that you will be wearing that suit and tie at meetings with them. If you're going to try to sell your services, and you do have to, attorneys and corporate personnel will talk to the man in the suit and tie and will be more ready to believe the man in the suit and tie before the guy in flannel and blue jeans. Image does count. A discussion as to whether it should or not is unnecessary because it does. Your use of the English language should go beyond simple or sounding pretentious. Speak plainly but professionally. If you want to impress clients, do it. Technical jargon from *their* profession will. Knowing claims-related language, legal terminology, civil and criminal law and procedure, recent court decisions, corporate accounting, etc. will be more likely to impress people.

Because reports are considered our product, remember that a product also needs a professional presentation. No, it doesn't have to be a leather-bound, gold-trimmed file that you give to your client. Particularly for lengthier, more complicated investigations (fraud investigations, for instance), having the report in some type of folder or cover will make a difference. Even in this line of work, it is the little things that clients remember as much as whether or not the case is "solved." Regular phone calls to the client making them aware of the status of the investigation can give you that edge also.

A final note in this brief "chapter." This chapter is restrained, concise, direct, or whatever you might want to say for a reason. Brevity is appreciated by most people, and, though there are volumes and volumes written on ethics and professionalism, the basic precepts are not difficult to grasp. Ultimately, no matter how much discourse we might put forth, the result will still be determined on an individual basis.

CHAPTER EIGHT

A Word, or Two, on Report-Writing

Probably everyone's least favorite subject, report-writing, does require some attention. Those who think that private investigations is a way to escape from the tediousness of paperwork need to think again. Particularly in the case of surveillance, undercover operations, shopper-testing, and fraud investigations, the "private sector" quite regularly writes at least twice as much as law enforcement. And, although some would argue, a good investigator who can't write reports is often less valuable than an average investigator who writes exceptional reports.

Too Much Detail? Despite what anyone might tell you, there is no limit to the detail you should initially put in your reports. *Always make copies of your original, unedited report.* A simple idea is that information can always be taken out of a report if it is unnecessary, but it can't be added afterwards. Continually adding addendums, using follow-up investigative action reports or other such measures can only be done when the client is aware that the investigation is on a continuing basis. Most clients expect that the report you submit is complete as to the subjects it is supposed to cover.

Some Simple Rules
Reports are written for the reader. The reason that reports are edited is because most people are not capable of proofing their own work. The author knows what he intends to convey, even if that is not what's on the paper. The reader will eventually be your client, who will want as much spelled out as clearly, concisely, and professionally as possible. Your report should

allow the reader to develop a picture of the events of the investigation, as well as knowing what information was obtained.

Reports should be thought of as evidence. Your reports will be used, in conjunction with any video or photographic evidence obtained, to prove or disprove something. Quite often, attorneys will present these reports to the "opposing" attorney, who will then decide what action is best in regards to the likelihood his client has a leg to stand on. At least fifty percent of the time, if your report is well-written, the other side will back down, and you won't have to worry about testifying. With a workers' compensation case, for instance, your attorney will most likely present the report and video to the claimant's attorney outside of the arbitration hearing initially. If both are done well, the claimant may experience a miraculous recovery.

Reports are your product. With the exceptions of service of process, bail enforcement, and some locates, your reports will be the second basis of judgment of your work a client has. Obviously the work needs to be done, in that the information needs to be obtained. Successfully performing the investigation is the first half, accurately reporting the success is the second.

Reports are written in a third person, narrative style. With the possible exception of undercover reports, all reports should be written using a third person, narrative style. Undercover reports, although not everyone that you might work for would agree, are best written using your first name, and the initial of your last name, making you appear to be the subject under observation.

Most reports are written:

    7:00a.m.   The reporting investigator arrive at 1229 Birch . . .
                  or,
    7:00a.m.   Investigator #0061/2 arrive at 1229 Birch . . .

The idea is that you don't use your name but rather a third person, objective subject of the sentence. Neither would any of the following be used: I, we, me, etc. Different agencies will have different words that they want you to use (investigator, agent, etc.), and that is hardly important. The idea here is to reinforce the idea that a professional, objective observer was present, and to keep your name out of it until it becomes necessary for people to know who the reporting investigator was. And, there is a good possibility each time your report is well-written that no one will ever have to know because the other side recognizes how professional of an investigator you are and therefore doesn't want you in court testifying.

Undercover reports can be written:

> 7:00a.m.   Ed H. was observed entering the employee entrance.

With the report written in this fashion, Ed H. being the undercover operative, if the unusual were to happen and somehow the "bad guys" got hold of the reports, they would now be inclined to believe that Ed H. is being investigated. Depending upon how well the U.S. agent has done his or her job, the "bad guys" might even warn him. The likelihood that the reports will get to anyone other than their intended reader is slim to none, but, now you're prepared even for that contingency.

You're not in the military, and neither are your clients. Although reports **are** written in chronological order, generally speaking, they **are not** written using the military/twenty-four hour time clock. Yes, your report should reflect the time you started, and each entry should then come in the chronological order in which it occurred, but it is rare that a client will want to have to convert 1900hrs to seven o'clock. It simply is not something a client will want to have to do in addition to absorbing the material contained in the report. Unless specifically told otherwise by a supervisor, the appropriate format is **a.m.** or **p.m.**

Formal, fluff, filler and lies. There is a world of difference between formal, fluff, filler, and lies. If a supervisor or a client should want you to alter a report, you better have the ability to say no. Don't be surprised if a client wants you to put in a few additions to a report. Clients are not always angels themselves. Can you live with lying while under oath? Do you want to live with the embarrassment of contradicting your own report while in a courtroom? *Formal* writing is what you should always be attempting to achieve. You will probably find people in this industry who will refer to this as fluff. Total mastery of the English language is not necessary, but the ability to go beyond simple sentences, to use a collegiate vocabulary at least some of the time, and to communicate effectively at various levels is important. *Fluff and filler* is the unnecessary use of descriptive detail, reporting on observations irrelevant to the investigation, or the substitution of a "twenty-five-dollar" word when it is not appropriate or necessary. They can be harmless as long as they do not alter the implications of the report, and they do not contain lies. And, while some clients might tell you they want simple, direct reports, they will be the same clients who ask why the report for four hours of uneventful surveillance is only one page long. **Do not lie within any report,** but, it is not necessarily unheard of to use a little filler or fluff to satisfy the client who has shown that the length of a report will help his mind justify the expense of the investigation.

Something not to say.

> 7:00a.m.   Nothing happened at the location, or No activity.

Outside of the obvious fact that this looks lazy and less than professional, it also leaves you wide open for a good attorney if you get called into court (that is a distinct probability if your report is written in this fashion). Given this entry in a report, the attorney for the opposing side can ask you what you mean by "nothing happened." Or, more likely, he can introduce the facts that at seven a.m. on that morning; the paperboy dropped off *The Daily Herald*, the neighbor was walking his dog, his client was in the middle of preparing breakfast, his client's wife was getting the children ready for school. Then, he asks you if all of those things would be considered activities, events, or things that were actions and, therefore, happened. Then he'll say something along the lines of, "therefore mister investigator, were you lying within your report, or were you at the wrong address on the morning in question?"

What you should write. Because there will be many times when there is little to no activity visible to you, especially if you work for an agency who is primarily involved with surveillance investigations, this needs to be addressed.

> 7:00a.m.   No visible signs of activity were observed at the subject's residence.

This qualifies that the investigator observed no activity, nor visible signs of activity, at the subject's residence. It does not make any statements outside the scope of the investigator's ability to observe (remember, *observing doesn't only mean seeing*). And, this is one of the most important things to remember about reports:

Only reporting your observations while out on the assignment. While there will be exceptions to this rule, your habit should be to leave opinions, deductions, conclusion, etc. out of the report. They should be reserved for conversations with the client. It does not matter the years of experience you've had, nor the fact that you're right; in a report, facts are all that are important. There will be times, particularly with fraud related investigations, other than workers compensation fraud, when a client will want you to express an opinion within the context of a report. When you do so, just to cover yourself, make sure that you also state that it is an opinion and requires further investigation for documentation as fact.

About descriptions. Different agencies will probably have different requirements in relation to descriptions. As is the nature of any work in this industry, adapt to the circumstances, of your immediate assignment. At the end of this chapter, there are sample reports. You may find yourself working for someone who disagrees with the format and/or other aspects of these reports. Especially if you are operating in a state that, like Illinois, requires that you work for an agency for a minimum period of time prior to being eligible to test for your own license, write your reports the way the boss wants. What is important to remember about descriptions is that you should use enough detail to specifically identify the subject, reflect only the facts as you observed them during the investigation, and **get used to using the word approximately.** Again, there comes the question of the attorney for the opposing side if you should get called into court.

For instance, while on a surveillance, you opt to use this description of the subject:

> White male, 5'8", 165', 32 y.o.a., brown hair, a black and gray flannel shirt, blue jeans, and steel-toed, work-type boots.

The clever young attorney will approach and ask if the description he just read was the description you provided of his client on that day and time in question, You reply, "yes sir." He replies, "interesting. And, I say interesting because at that time on that day in question my client was in fact thirty-three years of age, has been five foot seven for all his adult life, and has not weighed less than one hundred and seventy pounds for the last fifteen years. So, mister detective, the question is whether you were lying in the context of your report, or were you watching the wrong person that day?"

Again, this does not make you look good. And, while it might not win the case for the other side, you want to leave them as few avenues to question your credibility as possible. Writing a report that leaves little to no room for doubt is perhaps the easiest way to do that. Even if you do have the person's vital statistics, your report reflects your observations, not your knowledge. **Approximately** is what anyone, no matter how well trained or experienced, observes.

So, instead we have:

> White male, approximately, 5'8", 165', 32 Y.O. A., brown hair, etc., etc.

Other important information in reference to descriptions of persons: Hair style (especially if balding), glasses, scars, marks, tattoos, jewelry. **Distinguishing features** is a general category for those features that are particular to the individual, vehicle, or building. With people, a missing limb, for instance, would be an important distinguishing feature. Believe it or don't, I have seen people forget to mention that little aspect of a description.

Other important information in reference to descriptions of vehicles: **Approximate** year, make, model, license plate, # of doors, color, distinguishing features. The first six items would be what is normally expected. In this line of work, you may run into instances when you are able only to get a quick glance at a vehicle. With a quick glance, you will obviously get the color. Of next concern should be license plate. Yes, people can switch plates, but that risk is unavoidable. The model becomes next most important because if you see that the person was driving a Blazer, you know or can easily find out the name of the manufacturer. *Distinguishing features* can range from the vehicle identification number (not easy to obtain under normal circumstances when you are trying not to be noticed), to rust, dents, luggage rack, bumper stickers, etc.

Other important information in reference to descriptions of building structures: Address, number of stories, color, type of construction (brick, frame, etc.), type of building (single family home, multi-unit office complex, etc.), number and location of exits, attached and/or detached structures, *distinguishing features* (that can include anything from the placement of the mailbox in relation to others in adjacent buildings, construction being done, architectural style, lawn ornaments, etc.).

Direction and location within the report. It should become habit that whenever you refer to something in a report in the sense of direction (left or right), or location (front, back, rear, stern, aft, etc.) that will immediately be followed by the compass direction:

... the subject then proceeded to make a left, turning southbound on Main

... a gray metal tool shed, approximately 5'0" in height and four feet wide, was located to the left (west) of the residence.

... the subject was seen exiting the back (south) door of the building.

Reports do not make the investigator, but they do make the difference between the investigator who gets by and the successful investigator, in most cases. They are a means of communication and a form of evidence, and they need to be treated as such. Service of process, bail enforcement, and sometimes other types of locate investigations will not often require full, formal reports. And, you can earn a decent living doing any of those. But, as much fun as any type of investigation might be, eventually everything becomes boring. So, if you opt to adopt the belief that "real detectives" don't worry about fancy reports or some similar macho, testosterone-induced approach, be prepared to be limited to certain types of work and certain types of clients.

CHAPTER NINE

Recommended Reading

As was stated at the beginning and probably restated too much, this book does not pretend to be a book that will *make you a private investigator.* If someone tries to say his or her book or video-tapes will make you a private investigator, and you believe it, I've got a recently refurbished bridge for sale. Neither does this book provide lists of "public access" information sources. Others have done that. This book approaches private investigations from a practical, realistic perspective, offering information in plain language, not technical jargon. The reason that this recommended reading chapter exists is because others have amassed lists and put together "complete guides" that have their place. The truth about private investigations is that not everyone will be good at it. It is like any other profession: you can have one hundred people read the same books, study the same materials, and take the same tests—even if they all get one hundred on the test, they won't all make good detectives. Whether you call it *mindset, personality, character,* or anything else, some people just don't make it. But, if our industry is going to grow as much as the experts say, we're going to need a lot more people trying.

There are probably as many books on various subjects within private investigations as there are fictionalized books about private investigations. No matter what your line of work is, no matter why you're reading, you *can't* read too much. Unless of course, all you do is read. Then you might run into some problems with creditors, bosses, and other people who want you to get up out of your chair and earn some money. And, in this line of work in particular, no matter how much you read, you need exposure to "the streets," even if the streets are not the down and dirty ones. *Reclusive* is an adjective I've never known to be associated with a good detective.

If you plan to be an exceptional detective, you should also be reading history books, business books, and writing books along with the standard fare. And, you should take advantage of any opportunity to attend seminars or classes that specifically address conducting certain types of investigations or related areas. Remember, as an investigator you'll need to be a jack of many trades and a master of one.

As a last note, don't take this recommended reading list as the complete list. There are far too many books written for any one person to read. Your thirst for knowledge should be unquenchable; your desire to learn insatiable.

Some suggestions to have in your library.

How to Locate Anyone Who Is or Has Been in the Military (Armed Forces Locator Directory) by Lt. Col. Richard S. Johnson
MIE Publishing, Post Office Box 340081, San Antonio, TX, 78234

How to Find Almost Anyone, Anywhere
by Norma Mott Tilman
Rutledge Hill Press, 211 Seventh Avenue, North Nashville, TN, 37219-1823

How to Make $100,000 A Year As A Private Investigator
by Ed Pankau
Cloak & Data Press, Inc, P.O. Box 2484, Onalaska, TX, 77360

How to Market Your Private Investigation Business (A Practical Guide for the Serious P.I.)
by Bob Mackowiak
available through P.I. Magazine

You, Too, Can Find Anybody
by Joseph J. Culligan
Hallmark Press, Inc., 1337 N.W. 155th Drive, North Miami, FL, 33169

Other books to have on hand.

- Your state's Criminal Law and Procedure book
- Your state's Civil Code and Procedure book

- *Roget's Thesaurus*
- *Webster's* Complete, Unabridged Dictionary
- *Ballantine's Law Dictionary*
- *Black's Law Dictionary*
- *Sullivan's Law Directory*

Subscriptions worth maintaining.

- *The Wall Street Journal*
- *P.I. Magazine*
- *Time*
- *Newsweek*
- At least one of your local papers
- Your local county's bar brief. (Being an associate member of the Bar Association *is* a good idea.

A related area.

Membership to certain organizations is a subject to be addressed also; it is addressed within the context of this chapter because what most of these memberships have to offer is a monthly publication with useful information, as well as assisting you to network professionally.

- A.D.I. (for those practicing in Illinois): the Associated Detectives of Illinois
- Chiefs of Police Association
- A.S.I.S.: the American Society of Industrial Security Specialists (This organization in particular is recognized as providing worthwhile training programs that provide certifications—C.P.P., certified protection professional—that are respected.)
- National Association of Investigative Specialists: an organization that will soon be for investigations what A.S.I.S. is to security
- Your local Chamber of Commerce
- Your local Bar Association

As was discussed in reference both to locate and undercover investigations, there is no proven formula for what you should know. The best private detectives are people who have a wealth of information on a variety of subjects. The more you can learn, the better you will become. And, because most of us can't afford to perpetually take college courses or attend every seminar that comes along, *read as much as you can.* Working with other investigators, especially more seasoned ones who have worked a variety of cases, is a good option too. But, there you are subject to the willingness of the detective to share his methods, insights, and experience. There are those of us who believe that by helping newcomers in the field we strengthen ourselves and help our profession gain the respect it deserves, but there are also those who feel differently.

CASE FILES: Bringing a Family Back Together

It had been over a month since I had had a call to conduct an undercover or attempt to locate any fugitives. In certain ways, the break was sort of nice. I had been doing some process service background and light skip-trace work. The bills were still getting paid, and I actually had a relatively normal life for a little while. When the call came in that day for the case, I felt even better that I would be the person taking it.

"I spoke to Richard," the woman on the phone said. "And he told me to call back. I've tried to get as much information together as I could."

"Relax, Mrs. Hernandez," I said, intentionally keeping my voice at a low, slow, calming pitch rate. "Meet me in a half hour at the Shoney's, and we'll go over everything."

My partner Rich had told me about the case. It was a sixteen year old runaway. Rich's specialty was corporate investigations—undercovers, background, financial. Outside of undercovers, I had spent most of my time in the private sector and as a Military Police Officer doing skip-trace/locate work. In the M.P. Corps, I had worked a variety of investigations that required heavy locate work. Of course, a lot of that work had been locating fugitives from justice or fugitives from financial obligations, and only a few cases had been of this nature. I had conducted a small number of adoption investigations and a similar number of missing persons cases. Helping a family to find their sixteen year old runaway daughter was the type of case I preferred to work. There was always the possibility of failure or finding out something no one wants to know, but in this particular instance, it seemed as if the daughter was only beginning to be led astray by the wrong people. I felt there was a strong probability of a successful locate and a relatively happy reunion.

I made a couple of quick calls to let people know where I would be and walked out to my car. Unlike the television private investigators, I had an "average" car. It was a maroon Toyota Tercel, two door, with a dent in the right, front fender. Gray primer marked the point of impact and also made the car a bad choice for a surveillance vehicle. Anything from a dent to a sport stripe to a bumper sticker that individualized a vehicle increased the likelihood that someone would remember that particular vehicle. For undercovers it had the effect of adding to my down and out image. In reality, I hadn't been able to have the repairs done because I couldn't afford to have the car in a shop for a week. In our line of work, a telephone and a vehicle were absolute necessities. And, while I could afford a rental, I preferred to wait for a slow work period. Most rental places had restrictions on taking the vehicle out of town, and mileage costs were ridiculous. I got in and started the car up. I patted the dashboard; I had put the car through quite a bit of abuse, and it had never quit on me.

After speaking with Mrs. Hernandez, I was even more confident that we would be successful. She had a complete list of her daughter's regular contacts, including the boyfriend, who was the obvious trouble spot. He was a twenty-two year old male with a previous conviction for drug trafficking. He had known gang affiliations and was currently going to trial over a stolen auto charge involving our client. Of course, it was probably true that her daughter had gotten the keys for him, but she had made demands for the return of the auto, and he had refused. The only real reason that the local law enforcement might try to work with him was that he could probably give them a substantial amount of information regarding gang and drug activity. Considering that the runaway was an un-emancipated minor, however, he would be an easy squeeze regarding her location.

Mrs. Hernandez had also told us that her daughter was due a check from her work, which she had not been showing up to. She was due to pick up the check the day after next, so I had told our client we would not start the heavy locate work until after that day. After all, if the daughter or friend showed up to pick up the check, we stood a good chance of closing the case right there. And, besides closing the case quicker and reuniting the family, it would substantially decrease the hours involved and, therefore, the cost.

After our meeting, I contacted our best female investigator, informed her of the situation, and explained the time on Friday that we would need to be present at the store. Outside of the fact that Monica was a female and would be needed on this, she was a dependable street investigator. I had enough other business to keep me busy, so I told Monica to meet me at the location in Schaumburg at ten. The store would not release checks until ten, but I would be there at nine to talk to the loss prevention people and the store manager. I knew that they would not want anything to occur on their property, and I would not want anything going down in the store either. There were too many variables. It was safer, easier, and more readily controlled if we waited until she was out of the store. All I would want the store personnel to do would be to call the local police.

"I'm sorry," the man in the gray, pin-striped suit said. "That is simple the policy according to our corporate legal offices. We cannot allow anything to occur here. We cannot get involved in any way."

"I'm not asking you to get involved in any way," I explained again. "I wouldn't want anything to happen in your store. I want to wait until she's out of the store. I'm simply asking that we be allowed to have an investigator inside the store so we can follow the girl out. Then, you could call the Schaumburg police and tell them a run-away just came in and picked up her check. We've already checked in with them; they know the situation."

"I'm sorry," the woman I had first spoken to said. "We simply can't do anything. All we're legally allowed to do is put a note in her check envelope telling her to call her mother. We can't attempt to stall her in any way."

"Do you have any children, ma'am?" I asked, beginning to let my anger show a little.

"Whether she has any children or not is none of your business," the man in the suit said. "And, I would appreciate it if you would leave now." I looked at both of them. I looked into their eyes, trying to see past the corporate façade. As I turned away, I wondered. If Bram Stoker were correct, and the eyes were the windows to the soul, had these windows always revealed a completely empty view?

"Well, they know what you look like. But they haven't seen me," Monica said, and her impish grin started at the corners of her mouth.

"How very true. Okay. You try to keep shopping around, and I'll hang around the front of the mall. If she comes in, you'll have to make the call on how to handle it."

"Do my best."

Thanks to the corporate legal department, no one's best would do any good under these circumstances. There were six possible entrances to the store at One Schaumburg Place, meaning we would need six pair of eyes to watch them, another two people to watch both the front and rear of the building, and someone waiting to call the Schaumburg police if the runaway arrived. I had a cellular phone, but I could only be in one place at a time. And because we couldn't even be sure the girl would show up, much less an approximate time, it was impossible for the Schaumburg police to let a unit loose just to assist us. Police departments often got the blame under these circumstances; it was the corporate conscience that deserved it.

The girl did show up to pick up her check. Monica had managed to befriend one of the female loss prevention agents by that time and had sent her to inform me of the runaway's presence. Much as I suspected, however, the girl had a car waiting around the corner. Monica was following her out of the store at a reasonable distance, but as soon as the girl got out of the store, she ran around the corner. It would have been impossible for anyone to maintain the tail and get the car info. Monica and I departed the area very aggravated. We met with our client later that day, and discussed our plan of action. We were going to have to hit the streets and begin standard skip-trace/locate procedures. Luckily for us, the client had a large number of leads. Monica and I wanted to talk to the ex-con boyfriend first; he had a lot to lose by associating with a minor, especially if it could be proven that he was harboring a runaway. It was four o'clock when we arrived at the residence of the boyfriend. His family name was not listed on the board for the apartment, but we buzzed it anyway. No answer. As we were walking out, two young men came walking in.

"Yo Johnny," I called, hoping to get a response.

"What up?" the older, tougher looking young man said.

"You are," Monica responded and showed him her badge. "We're private detectives, and we need you to tell us where we can find two runaway's".

"Look mang," he responded, leaning up against the rail, "I don't need no trouble. I tol' that girl to go back home. I even wrote her mother a letter sayin' she was gonna be doin' this if her mother don't let up on her. She show you that?"

"She sure did. And that was a very nice touch. Now, let me tell you minor. If we can't turn her up soon, I'm sure somebody's going to want to know about your relations with her. And if this has to go to the police, and they find out you knew where she was, well, they can create a lot more trouble for someone with a record than we can." Monica had children of her own. And one thing I had learned a long time ago doing this type of work: mothers have an entirely different attitude about people when it comes to any situation involving children. No matter what circumstances, a mother always knew and always cared about her child.

"We, on the other hand, disappear as soon as the girl is back with her family," I said, knowing that we would cooperate in any way if law enforcement wanted to pursue any of the possible charges that he might face in relation to the runaway situation. "We don't have any authority or obligation to do anything."

"You tell her mom to leave me alone if I help you find her?"

"We can talk to her about it," Monica said.

"Look, all I know is, las' time Mary—that's the other girl—las' time she ran away, she was stayin' up in one the hotel's 'round there."

"Well, let's hope she is this time too," I said and took a card out of my pocket. "You hear anything different, though, you get a hold of me. That's got my pager number on the back."

"Let's hope she is, and we get this wrapped up right away. I really don't want to talk to you again." Monica wasn't mincing any words with him. I really didn't want to give him my pager number, but it was necessary. He was the kind of person who might prove useful as an informant on other cases. Our client had had my pager going off almost every other hour with new ideas, but that was ordinary.

Many times, when doing this type of work, the investigator doubled as a counselor. It was a job that I wasn't necessarily qualified for but I learned a great deal about over the years. People needed someone to talk to, someone to throw their thoughts and ideas at, and someone who was aware of the situation. You had to walk a fine line between being comfortable and encouraging false hopes if the investigation wasn't going well. I did not envy the counselors who had to handle cases that had a greater likelihood of negative results. Because we had the ability to concentrate our attention on cases, when people contacted us prior to law enforcement, we were often successful. Normally, the longer a person waited, the less likely they were to locate a runaway.

Monica and I spent the rest of that day contacting some of the friends, and stopping at the surrounding hotels. We left a business card with my pager number, and a description of the two girls at each hotel. We hoped that, even if they had already checked in, the personnel at the hotels would be more cooperative than the personnel at the place where our girl had worked. And we knew that they were more likely to be cooperative because they didn't want any minors getting rooms at their establishments.

It was seven-thirty Sunday morning when my pager went off. I didn't recognize the number, so I knew it wasn't our client. I felt a sense of relief, immediately followed by a sense of guilt. I got up, went to my desk, and dialed the number.

"Good-morning, motel seven," a voice answered.

"I hope it is a good morning. My name is Jim Edwards. Someone just paged me."

"Oh, yes sir. It was I. The girls you look for. I believe they are here. But, I am not sure. A young man checked in yesterday, and I saw those girls, but I get off before you come here."

"We'll be right there."

"Do you want that I should talk to them?"

"No, don't do anything. Just leave them alone. My partner and I will be there in a half hour."

I called Monica and told her where to meet me. If anyone were going to approach two teenage runaway girls in a hotel room, it was going to be Monica. I wouldn't even go up, except that the person that signed the room out might be there and less than friendly. And, while Monica could certainly take care of herself, it was always better to avoid those types of problems by presenting the most difficult challenge. It was similar to having a shotgun for home protection: when threatened by a shotgun there was little possibility of resistance. When confronted by Monica and a male partner, there was little likelihood of resistance. And, for a wide variety of reasons, I always preferred no trouble to overcoming trouble.

Monica stood in front of the door and knocked. One of the girls answered, asking who it was. When Monica responded that it was Monica and she wanted to speak to our runaway, the door was opened slowly. Monica had taken the chance that our runaway knew her, and it had paid off. As it turned out, they were in the room, alone. While Monica explained to the girls what would be happening, I went down to the front desk. I instructed the manager to call the Arlington Heights police and report a runaway minor at her location. I talked to the man who had seen the girls, and he provided me with a description of the young man who had checked in and gotten the room. He also gave me the check in the paper that the young man had filled out in order to get the room. I didn't know whether or not charges were going to be pursued, but I wanted to give the police everything they would need as soon as they arrived. Being a typical Sunday morning in the quiet suburb of Arlington Heights, the police were at the front door by the time I had finished talking to the front desk clerk. They were slightly suspicious at first. That was normal for the Chicago Metro area. Law enforcement and private investigators had a shaky history. I knew there were people at fault on both sides of the line; I had worked both sides.

I had no way of changing the reputation that private investigators had gotten due to certain celebrity investigators from Illinois, but I had found that your own reputation was the line. I had no way of changing what preceded you, and, therefore, decided the level of cooperation and respect you were given. By the time Monica and I left the station that morning, we both had another officer who understood that not all private investigators were simply sleazes taking advantage of other people's miseries. As we were driving away, though, I couldn't stop the anger I felt for the company that couldn't even call the police. In a country like ours, it disgusted me that lawyers, liabilities and lawsuits dictated the actions people took even under these type circumstances. Monica felt the same way. It was nothing either of us was going to change. As I lit another Winston, I thought it was probably a major contributing factor to my continued support of the tobacco industry.

CASE FILES: A Pretext is Worth a Thousand Databases

It has been said, in reference to writing, that a picture is worth a thousand words. Just as apt a saying, in relation to many types of investigations, but locate investigations in particular, is the title of this case file. Having performed numerous locates over the last fifteen years, ranging from working on the United States Army Military Police Corps AWOL Apprehension Team, to bounty-hunting, to adoption searches, runaway, and others, I have found it most often true that people, not computers, will find those subjects who are actually trying to hide. For simple locates, those subjects whose actual records can be located through public access sources or phone directories, etc., databases are wonderful. But, far too much emphasis is put on these, and I am sure I could find a number of people who would agree that, if you don't have people skills, common sense, and some imagination, you'll only be able to locate those people anyone who is computer literate could.

"Well," I said, putting my coffee cup down and picking up the pack of Winston's lying on top of the case file on my desk, "I guess we better start with the obvious first."

"Are you driving?" Danni asked and stood up. "Because if I am, you better give me at least fifteen minutes to move my back seat to my trunk."

"Why don't you go ahead and get started," I replied, lighting the cigarette I had taken out, "My ride's still trashed from camping this weekend."

Having worked closely with Danni for almost six months, I knew what she meant when she said she had to move her back seat to her trunk. She was quite often carrying half of her worldly possessions around with her; her "gypsy lifestyle" as she put it. Rumors about Danni and me flew around the office quickly, but there was no truth to them. As much as Danni's "gypsy" lifestyle appeared to be that of the stereotypical "free-spirit," she was also a very old-fashioned, Italian Catholic. And, despite the fact she and I had been out on long surveillance and other assignments together, it wasn't straight out of a Hollywood scene. We mostly traded sarcastic quips, exchanged bad puns, or practiced pretext "voices."

By the time Danni had gotten back into the office, I had called the service I sometimes use for more difficult locates. I was inclined to use them sparingly, as most of the information sources they tapped I could check myself, but they were quicker, relatively cheap, and had a couple of sources I couldn't get to. The information they produced normally wasn't where my subject was actually located, but it was good reference information about past addresses, and places I could go to talk to people.

"Ready to head down to LaSalle?" Danni asked, pretending one of her favorite southern drawls.

"Yes, ma'am," I answered, standing up and getting my jean jacket on, "Reckon that'd be the place to be goin'."

"You have to work on that," Danni said, walking out, "You do a better inner-city slang than anyone I know, but you're too Texas on your southern. Our boy's from Mississippi."

"Workin' on it, ma'am," I responded, closing and locking the door behind us.

Our "boy" was Timmy Meyer, who had jumped bail on fraud and theft by deception charges in Georgia. He was originally from Illinois, but his parents had divorced when he was seven, and he had moved with his mother to Mississippi. He still had family in Illinois, and that was how we wound up on his trail. None of the information that he had supplied to the bail bondsman was accurate, but that was hardly a surprise. In Timmy's case, it may not have even been intentional. It had been over twenty years since he had moved to Mississippi.

It was a little over an hour to the LaSalle County Courthouse, and while Danni was driving, I spent the time getting my week in order. We had Timmy to work on and had gotten two more locate requests over the weekend. One was another bail enforcement case, and the other was a deadbeat parent. Most of the detectives I associated with would rather do a week of surveillance than the types of locates and backgrounds I did, but then again, most of them could never understand how I had thought that undercover operations were fun.

"I'll check the criminal," I said, as we stepped through the doors to the LaSalle County Courthouse. "You check the civil."

"Sir, yes sir," Danni replied, mockingly military. My stock response to that was that she shouldn't call me sir because I worked for a living. I had been an enlisted soldier when I was in military police officer, and it was the standard response every non-commissioned officer gave when called sir.

Danni hadn't been in the military, and while she possessed more self-discipline and attention to detail than a lot of soldiers I met the MP Corps, she never understood the need for rigorously enforced discipline. While I understood the military motivations for actions, I had gotten out because it wasn't making sense for me anymore.

"My," Danni said, walking up behind me, "apparently he's been busy around here also?"

"A few years back, though," I answered, handing her a couple of the files I had already gone through. "Looks like he was here and gone after he got everything taken care of."

"Including his ex-wife," Danni added, not looking up from the file she was reading. "Seems like marriage was a little too much stability for him."

"Well, at least he's got something figured right," I answered, waiting for Danni's reply.

She was married and very much an advocate of the married life. She had been trying to convince me for the last eight months we had been working together that, as long as you were careful and both of you were being honest, marriage was great. Sometimes I talked to her about it honestly, and a lot of times I was sarcastic or would argue points just for fun, but I tried not to let her know that was that. Just bringing up the idea that marriage was a myth perpetrated by the Catholic religion was enough to get her going, especially because she knew I had been raised, but had stepped away a number of years ago.

"Not in the mood for debates right now," Danni replied. "Did you see this address on Scott? It was in the papers the bondsman sent us."

"That's why two heads are better than one," I reluctantly admitted. Danni had awoken me to the fact I had gotten into a rut a few months back. The "powers of observation" much vaunted in the P.I. industry were most often assumed to apply to being out on the street on surveillance, or as in the movies and television, at a murder scene or while talking to a suspect. And while it was true they were important in all cases, it applied to research, too. Somewhere along my eight years of experience, I managed to forget how many people I had made look incompetent just because I read the files more carefully. In a couple of locates, Danni had refreshed my memory to that fact. I had, as of that time, an even to this date, never been called to a murder scene right after the crime occurred. That is purely the stuff fiction is made of. "I guess I'll buy the coffee."

When we had gotten back to the office, the response from my computer information source connection was already faxed back. He had only been able to locate addresses we had already found as far as our man went. But, he did find another name and address off the social that we didn't. It was over six months old, but you don't write anything off until you personally verify or deny it. As I had learned early on in the business, the only way to know was to make sure for yourself. Though few people understood it, it wasn't as much a matter of trusting other people as it was a matter of human nature and society. A sufficient number of people know they'll get paid for a half-assed job, another group is overly confident that they've seen enough patterns to determine what must naturally follow, and there is that group that simply never learned the meaning of the phrase "work ethic." While it was true that most of the time certain assumptions were safe, the pay-off for checking instead of assuming had been good for me.

"So, research and data-bases have lead us to . . . ?"

"To knocking on doors," Danni said, putting down her cup of coffee and reaching over to grab the other case file that was on my desk. "I assume we're not doing that today?"

"I'll skip the obvious "assuming" crack."

"And I thank you for that."

"No, Timmy will wait until tomorrow, but we'll have to hit it hard. Read the file tonight; I don't think he's one to stay any place too long."

"Ten-four," Danni replied, and sat back reading the file. "Mind if I work on this guy for now?"

"Go ahead," I answered, turning my swivel chair to the computer on the side of my desk. "I've got a few affidavits to type up from this weekend."

"Putting off until tomorrow . . . ." Danni commented.

"Yes, mother," I replied in a nasal high-pitched tone.

"You know the FBI and a few other people are looking for this guy?"

"Doesn't surprise me," I answered, crushing my cigarette out in the ashtray on Danni's desk. When I had been on the Special Reactions Team in the Military Police, we had trained with the FBI's SWAT team, along with Border Patrol and the DEA. Other encounters with them were the reason one of my favorite lines from Men in Black was when Tommy Lee Jones said: "We're the FBI, ma'am. We don't have a sense of humor that we are aware of." They were definitely the best at computers, accounting and other uptight, white-collar crime investigations, but the lack of humor and imagination always amazed me. "The FBI is great for knocking on the door, waving their badge and assuming they can scare anyone into talking."

"How did I know you'd say something like that?" Danni asked jokingly.

"Well, I'm gonna try momma. Seems like it's worth a try."

"You know the Fed doesn't pretext anyone."

"I can't hardly believe that," Danni said. "But you probably know better than I do."

Danni put the file down and sat back in her chair. She was putting the pretext together in her mind. You never wanted to have any pretext so rigid that an unexpected question would noticeably throw you, but there was a certain amount of information that was important to keep fresh in your mind. As she picked up the phone, I anxiously lit a cigarette. Danni was one of the best when it came to pretexts that I had seen in years. Over the phone or in person, she played her role well.

"Hello," Danni said, pausing for a second, then resuming in her southern belle voice. "Hello, ma'am, is this 219-555-6794? . . . It is? Are you Timmy's mamma? . . . Well, it is so good to talk to you. Timmy told me so much about you . . . Me? Well, you mean Timmy didn't so much as mention me, ma'am? . . . Marianne, Marianne Jackson . . . Yes, ma'am, Jackson. We met in North Carolina, before Timmy got the job up in New York . . . . Well, I'm sorry, this is a little awkward. I just thought Timmy would have . . . . well, we don't have to talk if you don't . . . . I'm sorry, ma'am . . . Why yes, he said he was going to . . . . Well, what's wrong, mamma Meyers? You sound . . . . Is Timmy all right? . . . In prison? Good Lord. What for? I mean, Timmy does like to have fun, but he wouldn't ever hurt anyone . . . I just don't believe that mamma Meyers. Not Timmy. They probably set him up . . . I know, I know. Can I call him where he's at, or write to him or anything? . . . Well, I sure would like to write him . . . Yes, I know he's not much one for writing; he used to talk about that. Used to say how he hoped people didn't think he forgot about them . . . Yes, just let me get a pen."

Danni talked for a few minutes longer to Meyers's mother, talking about how Timmy was a good man, and she was sure he would get out quickly. I took the address she had written down and went into my office. After one information call and three calls through the New York prison system, I was able to determine that Meyers had been transferred to a minimum security facility after serving only three months at a stronger prison.

"How could they not find him?" Danni asked as she stepped into my office.

"Human error is inevitable everywhere," I replied. "Someone in the system typed his name, social security number or some other information wrong, so everyone assumed it was a different person. We have to bear in mind a little bit of luck on our part too. Not that Magnum or Mike Hammer would ever admit it, but luck cannot be ignored in the scheme of some successes."

"Well, that was easy money. Are you going to cut me the check today then?"

"Funny lady," I replied, standing up and walking out of my office. "Payday is payday. Now, go spend an evening with your hubby. We have a lot of work to do, and if we can get Timmy, we'll be on the road."

The next morning was a frustrating one. Despite the information we had obtained, there was little to no current information available about anyone we knew Timmy associated with or any family. I spent most of the morning on the phone back and forth with my computer information source. Danni had searched all over the internet for any sights that might be able to help, and no luck. Even the police department where Timmy had been arrested a few times had managed to lose all the records they had, so we had little to go on. What we had to work with was the address Danni had located the day before. It wasn't much, but either way we'd have to hit the street and knock on some doors anyway.

The address on Scott Street was relatively recent, four months old. We sat for an hour or two, hoping to see some coming and going. There was movement inside the apartment, but no one entering or exiting. I grabbed my herring-bone jacket out of the back and the small, black leather briefcase I used for professional pretexts. If Timmy was there, I'd play wrong apartment and go back to the car. If he wasn't, I'd be the insurance claim adjustor with a check that had to be signed by him. Luck was with us again, in the form of a couple of stoners who talked too much. I had to shift my pretext a little so I didn't appear too uptight, but they gave me quite a bit of information. Timmy hadn't lived there for awhile, but they knew he was living somewhere down in Ottawa. They thought maybe I could talk to his fiancée, who was working over at the Amoco restaurant just off of I-80. Amanda, something. They weren't really good at remembering last names. I wasn't really surprised by that admission.

We called before driving down to Ottawa. Amanda was schedule to work seven to two. We drove down right away, wanting to check in with local law enforcement to let them know what we were doing. Technically, the Sheriff's office would be the people to get involved, but on other occasions the LaSalle County Sheriff's office had declined, preferring to let us operate as bail enforcement personnel did in other states. In Illinois, that was not always the case. Having been a police officer, I always took the time to make the courtesy call. If we had to sit anywhere waiting for Timmy, at least if someone called us in as looking suspicious, the local coppers would know not to worry. After checking in, we had about two hours to kill, and we didn't want to send out any red flares by trying to find Timmy any other way. So, we made our way over to where the desk sergeant had told us the best cup of coffee was.

Amanda's personalized license plates were another luck factor that we hadn't counted on. As she pulled in, we noticed that she was alone. We had decided to get some dinner at the restaurant, and see if we could get some idea of Amanda's personality as she waited our table. If we got lucky, Timmy might even show up. That, we were not counting on.

INDEX OF QUESTIONS

Thefts. Almost every type of business suffers from theft of some kind. It can be small pilferage by individuals or a well organized ring stealing the client's product in terms of thousands of dollars. The following list will assist you in uncovering theft in the installation to that you are assigned. When theft is determined, keep in close contact with your supervisor. He will direct you in procedure and, if necessary, assign outside investigators to help you:

1. Have you observed employees taking client's products out of the plant during working hours?
2. Have you overheard any conversations regarding theft of any kind?
3. Can client's property be concealed in the trash? Have you checked it?
4. Are the employees placing any of the client's product in their lockers? If so, they may remove it from the company later.
5. Are the employees carrying out the client's product in their lunch pails, pocketbooks, or on their persons?
6. Do certain employees report early to work or remain after work? Determine why they are doing so.
7. Do employees complain about quotas, and is there a way they can falsify quotas?
8. Are there any rumors that employees on another shift are stealing?
9. Do any employees have outside friends visit them in the plant? Do former employees visit the plant?
10. Is there collusion between the truck drivers and plan employees? Note if the truck drivers are friendly with any particular employee.
11. Does the plant have a store where employees can purchase the client's property? Are the packages stamped or sealed? Can the

stamp or seal be duplicated? Is there a way this system can be used to commit theft?
12. Are all packages checked when employees leave the plant? Is this true only at quitting time or can a package be taken out during shift?
13. Can employees come and go as they please during their shift? Can they take client's property out through an unauthorized exit? Are they doing so?
14. Can client's property be thrown out a window by an employee to a waiting friend, or thrown out and picked up after work? Is this being done?
15. Does any particular employee go out to his car during the shift for any reason? Is he concealing client's property in his clothing or lunch pail?
16. Is company merchandise frequently left near exits? If so, try to watch it.
17. If client's merchandise is clothing, can it be worn by the thief?
18. How do employees handle the receiving of client's merchandise? Do they check the load? Are they careless?
19. Are all goods received taken inside or are some left on the receiving platform overnight? If so, is a recount made the following morning?
20. Are trucks loaded with client's product and left overnight? Are truck doors locked and sealed?
21. Do salesmen come in the plant for samples? Are they within their quota or constantly drawing samples?
22. Does the client have a guard force? Are they alert and doing their job? Do employees respect them?
23. Are any of the guards friendly with particular employees?
24. Do any of the employees drive expensive cars?
25. Have any employees mentioned they are living beyond their salaries?

Supervision. Client's supervisors are responsible for the controls within the plant. It is their responsibility that proper production is maintained, the quality of the product is satisfactory, and that those employees under their supervision obey the rules and regulations set down by the client. When the supervisors are lax in their duties, morale breaks down, controls do not function, and problems go undetected until inventory time. Remember that major thefts develop through small pilferage and small pilferage is often the result of poor supervision.

You should report on each supervisor individually. Your report should cover the following points:

1. Do the supervisors know their jobs?
2. Do they show favoritism?
3. Do they demand proper performance and work output from employees or are they lax in their job?
4. Are they like and respected by the employees and do they work well under their supervision?
5. Do they tolerate inefficiency or misconduct?

Employee activity. On your assignment you are to develop all the facts concerning matters in the client's establishment. While the specific problem is of first importance, you are to investigate thoroughly all other matters of importance. A report on the activities of the employees is of prime importance to the client in operating his business. Do not take it for granted that the client is already aware of certain irregularities because it is general knowledge, or the supervisor knows of it and does nothing about it. To assist you in this the following list is given for guidance:

1. Report the employee's attention to duties. Do they know their job, are they a good worker?
2. Report on any carelessness in the employee's performance of his duties.
3. Report on any breakage of imperfect work.
4. Report if employees overstay lunch or break periods.
5. Report on employees leaving the plant at odd times or making frequent trips away from the job. Try to determine where they go and what they do.
6. Report on employees leaving the plant through unauthorized exits.
7. Report on any time clock irregularities.
8. Report on how client's products are shipped. Are they misdirected? Does the client count his products being loaded? Does the counter do his job?
9. Report if the employees work fast to leave early or slowly to get overtime.
10. Report on anyone who talks of sabotage or damages the client's property.

11. Report on breakdowns of machinery or production, the cause, and how long it took to fix it.
12. Report on arguments or fights between employees, or animosity that interferes with their work.
13. Report on any inventories you seen taken, the method, and comments by the employees. Do you believe they are accurate?
14. Report on the efficiency and method production, and if there is a way to improve it.
15. Report if there are excessive rejections of material, the cause, and any corrective action taken.
16. Report on any drinking or gambling by employees.
17. Report on employees smoking in unauthorized areas.
18. Report on favoritism shown to certain employees.
19. Report on the training received by new employees, and attitude of older employees toward the newcomer.
20. Report on any employee who is doing a particularly good job or is trying to better himself.
21. Report on any employee not doing his job or who is a constant complainer.
22. Report on any employee who states he has a criminal record or was fired from another job.

Fire Hazards. Fire in an industrial plant can result in destruction of equipment, material, loss of lives and disfiguration. A plant can be totally destroyed by fire. It could mean tremendous loss to the client as well as putting employees out of work for months.

1. Report on any fire hazards observed.
2. Inspect fire extinguishers, fire hoses, and report on condition and when they were last inspected.
3. Are fire regulations observed?
4. Are fire doors closed at night?
5. Are sprinkler heads free of paint?
6. Is there any exposed electric wiring?

Shipping and receiving department.

1. Is there any unauthorized absence from the area?
2. Does the foreman dock supervisor overlook misconduct/breakage or idleness?

3. Do employees park their vehicles near the area?
4. Do employees leave early/overstay their lunch period, etc.
5. Is overtime incurred? Is it necessary?
6. Is all the merchandise returned inside the plant at night? Is any left out? Is any left near exits?
7. Is the area secured at night? Are loaded trucks locked and sealed?
8. Are keys left in any vehicles?
9. Does a supervisor check the area before departing?
10. Are loaded trucks re-checked in the morning?

Store investigations. The principles set forth in the preceeding check list/undercover guide will, in most cases, apply to your assignment in retail stores. There are other factors to look for peculiar to retail establishments. Besides employee theft, retail stores are plagued by shoplifters, both professional and amateur, adult and juvenile. The capture of shoplifters is the job of the store security department. It is not yours. However, you are expected to report on the proficiency of the security force. The investigation of retail store:

1. Are store detectives alert and active?
2. Extent of shoplifters activity.
3. Treatment of customers.
4. Are sales registers accurate and properly controlled?
5. Is there any drinking or drug abuse occurring?
6. Is favoritism shown by office personnel toward certain employees?
7. Are credit cards handled properly?
8. Are goods received properly counted and checked with invoice?
9. Are employees removing goods from the store?
10. Are goods marked down by the proper authority, i.e., salesperson marking down to sell to a friend?
11. Do salespersons damage goods purposely to obtain a markdown?
12. Are extra goods mailed out?
13. Are proper refunds given?
14. Do employees leave the store through unauthorized exits?
15. Are goods loaded on delivery truck checked against Invoice?
16. Is it possible to overload the truck, and is it being done?
17. Do employees get a discount? Do they buy for friends?
18. Are registers audited nightly?
19. Have there been complaints about lost credit cards?
20. Who cleans the store?

INDEX OF STATE REGULATORY AUTHORITIES

This list of state regulatory authorities should be double checked; as with state laws and regulations, changes are ongoing. A good investigator knows that anything related to government or law is subject to change or re-interpretation as least as frequently as there is an election—sometimes more frequently. In short, your ability to successfully conduct an investigation will not preclude the need to consistently check the laws and regulations.

State Name	For P.I. Licensing	More info
Alabama	None, requires business license	APIAon-line.com
Alaska	None, requires business license	akinvestigators.com
Arizona	Dept. of Public Safety, Licensing Division P. O. Box 6328 Phoenix, AZ 85005 (602) 223-2361.	aalpi.org
Arkansas	Arkansas Board of Private Investigators and Private Security Agencies #1 State Police Plaza Dr. Little Rock, Arkansas 72209 (501) 618-8600	

California	Licensing Division, Bureau of Security and Investigative Services 400 R Street Sacramento, CA 95814 (800) 952-5210	CALI-pi.org
Colorado	None	ppiac.org
Connecticut	Department of Public Safety, Division of State Police 294 Colony St. Meriden, CT 06450-2098	http://users.ntplx.net/calpi
Delaware	Detective Licensing, Delaware State Police P. O. Box 430 Dover, DE 19903 (302) 736-5900	
District of Columbia	Security Officers Management Branch, Metro Police Security Unit 2000 14th St. NW Washington, DC 20009 (202) 671-0500	
Florida	Florida Department of Agriculture and Consumer Services Division of Licensing, Bureau of License Issuance P.O. Box 6687 Tallahassee, Fla. 32314-6687 (850) 488-5381	fali.com
Georgia	State Board of Private Security Agencies 237 Coliseum Drive Macon, GA 31217-3858 (478) 207-1460	

Hawaii	Board of Private Detectives & Guards DCCA, PVL, Licensing Branch 1010 Richards St. P.O. Box 3469 Honolulu, HI 96801. (808) 586-3000 or (808) 586-2701	
Idaho	None	http://pial.us/
Illinois	Illinois Department of Professional Regulation 320 West Washington Street, 3rd Floor Springfield, IL 62786	
Indiana	Private Detective Licensing Board 100 N. Senae Ave., Rm 1021 Indiana Government Center North Indianapolis, IN 46204-2246 (317) 232-2980	
Iowa	Administrative Services Division, Iowa Department of Public Safety Wallace State Office Bldg. Des Moines, IA 50319 (515) 281-3211	iowa-investigators.com
Kansas	Kansas Bureau of Investigation 1620 SW Tyler Topeka, KS 66612 (785) 296-8200	k-a-l-i.org/
Kentucky	None	kpia.org
Louisiana	L.S.B.P.I.E. 2051 Silverside Drive, Suite 190 Baton Rouge, LA 70808	lpia.net
Maine	State Police Licensing Division State House Station #164 Augusta, ME 04333 (207) 624-8775	mlpia.org

Maryland	Maryland State Police, PI Licensing Division Jessup, MD (410) 799-0191, ext. 331	maryland-investigators.com misahq.com
Massachusetts	Massachusetts State Police Special Licensing Unit 485 Maple Street Danvers, MA 01923 978-538-6128 voice 978-538-6021 fax	lpdam.com
Michigan	The Department of Consumer & Industry Services P.O. Box 30018 Lansing, Michigan 48909 (517) 241-5645	mcpihome.com
Minnesota	Department of Public Safety Private Detective & Protective Agent Services Board 445 Minnesota St. St. Paul, MN 55101 (651) 215-1753	mapi.org
Mississippi	None	
Missouri	None	
Montana	Board of Private Security Patrol Officers and Investigators 301 S Park, Room 430 PO Box 200513 Helena, MT 59620-0513 (406) 841-2387, Fax: (406) 841-2309	
Nebraska	Secretary of State State Capitol, Suite 2300 Lincoln, NE 68509 (402) 471-2554	
Nevada	Office of the Attorney General Private Investigator's Licensing Board 100 N. Carson St. Carson City, NV 89701-4717 (775) 687-3223	

New Hampshire	State Police Division of Licenses and Permits Hazen DR., Concord, NH 03305 (603) 271-3575	
New Jersey	State Police Department of Law & Public Safety Private Detective Unit P. O. Box 7068 W. Trenton, NJ 08688-0068 (609) 882-2000, ext 2931	njlpia.com
New Mexico	Bureau of Private Investigators P.O. Box 25101 Santa Fe, NM 87504 (505) 476-7080	
New York	Department of State Division of Licensing Services 84 Holland Avenue Albany, NY 12208-3490	ldonys.org
North Carolina	Private Protective Services Board 1631 Midtown Place, Suite 104 Raleigh, North Carolina 27609 (919) 875-3611 (919) 875-3609 fax	ncapi.org
North Dakota	Private Investigative & Security Board P.O. Box 7026 Bismarck, ND 58505 (701) 222-3063	
Ohio	Ohio Department of Commerce Division of Licensing 77 South High St. Columbus, OH 43266-0546 (614) 466-4130	
Oklahoma	Council on Law Enforcement Education & Training Private Security Division P. O. Box 11476-Cimarron Station Oklahoma City, OK 73136-0476 (405) 425-2775	opia.com

Oregon	Oregon Board of Investigators 445 State Office Bldg. 800 NE Oregon Street #33 Portland, OR 97232 (503) 731-4359 FAX: (503) 731-4366	oali.org
Pennsylvania	None	pali.org
Puerto Rico	Policia De Puerto Rico GPO Box 70166 San Juan, PR 00936 (787) 793-1234	
Rhode Island	State of Rhode Island Providence Plantations 345 Harris Ave. Providence, RI 29221 (401) 277-2000	
South Carolina	State Law Enforcement Division Regulatory Services P. O. Box 21398 Columbia, SC 29221-1398 (803) 737-9000 Fax: (803) 896-7041	scalinu.com
South Dakota	None, requires business license	
Tennessee	Department of Commerce & Insurance Private Protective Services Division 500 James Robertson Parkway Nashville, TN 37243-1158 (615) 741-6382	tpia.com
Texas	Texas Commission on Private Security 4930 S. Congress, Suite C-305 Austin, TX 78745 P. O. Box 13509 Austin, TX 78711 (512) 463-5545 FAX: (512) 452-2307	tali.org

7Utah	Department of Public Safety & Law Enforcement Services Bureau of Regulatory Licensing 4501 South 2700 West Salt Lake City, UT 84119 (801) 965-4461	piau.com
Vermont	Board of Private Investigative and Armed Security Services Office of Professional Regulation 109 State St. Montpelier, VT 05609-1101 (802) 828-2837	
Virginia	Department of Criminal Justice Services Private Security Section P.O. Box 10110 Richmond, Virginia 23240-9998 (804) 786-4700	pisa.gen.va.us piaua.org
Washington	Department of Licensing, Public Protection Unit 405 Black Lake Boulevard P.O. Box 9649 Olympia, WA 98507-9649	wali.org
West Virginia	Secretary of State Licensing Division Private Investigator Licensing Charleston, WV 25301	
Wisconsin	Department of Regulation & Licensing P.O. Box 8935 Madison, WI 53708 (608) 266-0829	pawli.com
Wyoming	Local jurisdictions only.	

INDEX

A

ABC method   83, 84
adoption searches   27, 32, 36, 58, 139
advance work   91
attorney   14, 22, 31, 36, 43, 45, 48, 49, 51, 53, 59, 62, 64, 67, 107, 122, 124, 125

C

Citation to Discover Assets   41, 42
city hall   67
civil code   36
Civil Code and Procedure   10, 34, 44, 129
clients   10, 16, 22, 26, 41, 43, 45, 47, 48, 49, 50, 51, 54, 58, 59, 60, 64, 72, 74, 96, 101, 119, 121, 123, 127
Code of Civil Procedure   40
common sense   23, 24, 97
communication skills   *See* primary skills
County Clerk's Office   66
creativity   17, 24, 104
crime scenes   16
Criminal Defense   14
criminal justice   13, 26, 51
Criminal Justice   10, 34, 38, 51, 114
criminal law   36, 37, 119
curiosity   24

D

dead-beat parents   61
defendant   14, 47, 65
Department of Financial and Professional Regulation   8, 21, 68
Department of Professional Regulation   41
detective agency   9, 49, 74, 95, 96
distinguishing feature   126
Division of Professional Regulation   8, 21

E

entrapment   26, 99, 101, 106
executive protection   22, 28, 110
expectation of privacy   31, 35, 36, 58

F

firearm   8, 25, 28, 46
Freedom of Information Act of 1974   57, 63

Freedom of Information Request   67

I

individual license holder   9
interview   15, 25, 38, 63, 69, 71, 96
interview techniques   *See* interview
investigative techniques   9

K

knowledge   9, 16, 17, 18, 22, 24, 25, 26, 27, 29, 32, 34, 35, 38, 50, 57, 71, 74, 76, 78, 88, 97, 99, 109, 126, 129, 149

L

law enforcement   9, 13, 14, 16, 18, 24, 26, 27, 28, 30, 33, 38, 46, 51, 52, 54, 57, 60, 61, 72, 73, 80, 92, 94, 97, 99, 112, 113, 115, 118, 121, 133, 135, 136, 144
laws   8, 9, 16, 17, 26, 47, 57
license   7, 9, 10, 28, 30, 36, 41, 47, 48, 49, 51, 53, 62, 67, 68, 73, 74, 81, 86, 125, 126, 145
locate   22, 26, 30, 36, 47, 48, 49, 51, 58, 59, 61, 62, 63, 64, 65, 69, 73, 74, 77, 78, 127, 130, 132, 133, 135, 136, 139, 140, 141

O

operational definitions   21
Order   43
Orders of Protection   46

P

Paralegal   34
perjury   41
Permanent Employee Registration Card   21, 34
plaintiff   65
pocketing   101
police   14, 18, 38, 43, 51, 56, 60, 72, 92, 112, 113, 133, 134, 135, 137, 138, 140, 144
postal forwarding   46, 63, 69
pretext   29, 30, 31, 32, 33, 34, 52, 56, 63, 69, 88, 96, 97, 98, 100, 103, 106, 107, 110, 139, 142, 144
pretexts   8, 31, 33, 34, 143, 144
primary skills   22
private detective   8, 9, 10, 13, 15, 16, 17, 18, 19, 20, 27, 35, 36, 37, 40, 50, 51, 54, 58, 59, 60, 61, 68, 71, 72, 97
Private Detective   9, 20, 21, 57, 119
Private Detective Act   119
private investigations   8, 9, 10, 16, 18, 23, 24, 27, 34, 50, 56, 94, 121, 128
private investigator   8, 23, 104, 110, 128
privatization   26
process server's return   49

R

reasonable person standard   35
Recorder of Deeds   66
regulations   8, 9, 16, 20, 36, 41, 47, 50, 54, 98, 106, 148, 150
reports   22, 28, 41, 60, 79, 95, 96, 98, 99, 101, 103, 107, 108, 109, 119, 121, 122, 123, 124, 125, 127

report-writing   98, 104, 118, 121
report-writing skills   *See* primary skills
research skills   *See* primary skills

Rule to Show Cause   41, 42
runaway   19, 26, 27, 32, 61, 134, 135, 137, 139

S

scientific method   17
Secretary of State's Office   67
self defense   14
service of process   22, 40, 41, 43, 44, 45, 46, 47, 48, 49, 50, 56, 59, 78, 122
Service of Process   31, 59
skip-trace   47, 62, 132, 135
State's Attorney   41, 61
street sense   24
Summons and Complaint   23, 41, 42, 46
surveillance   7, 14, 18, 22, 29, 30, 40, 49, 59, 73, 74, 78, 79, 80, 81, 82, 83, 84, 85, 86, 87, 88, 89, 90, 91, 92, 110, 113, 121, 124, 125, 132, 139, 140, 141
  surveillance techniques   7
surveillance equipment   80

T

The Clerk of the Circuit Court   65, 66
theft   24, 28, 37, 95, 97, 100, 101, 105, 107, 109, 111, 117, 140, 147, 148, 151

tools   24, 27, 28, 99, 103
trash removal day   100

U

undercover   *See* undercover operations
undercover operations   10, 16, 18, 22, 26, 28, 30, 93, 94, 100, 112, 114, 115, 121, 140

V

vehicle   15, 28, 29, 47, 65, 67, 80, 81, 82, 90, 91, 92, 109, 113, 126, 132

W

Wage Garnishments   43
Wagner Act   107
workers' compensation   14